We Are Alike

A MEMOIR:

How a Doctor Leveraged

Her Neuroscience Expertise

to Survive and Heal

from Narcissistic Abuse

CAROL BETH NELSON, MD

Foreword by Rosalind Gold, MD

For information about this title or to order other books and/or electronic media, contact the editor:
Two Sisters Writing & Publishing®
TwoSistersWriting.com
18530 Mack Avenue, Suite 166
Grosse Pointe Farms, MI 48236

ISBN (Hardcover) 978-1-956879-97-1
ISBN (Paperback) 978-1-956879-98-8
ISBN (eBook) 978-1-956879-99-5

Printed in the United States of America
No part of this manuscript is fiction. Some names of people and places have been changed.
Book cover art and design: Illumination Graphics
Interior formatting: Illumination Graphics
Author photos: The Nelson Family Collection

Disclaimer

This is a work of nonfiction. While the events described are true to the best of the author's recollection, certain names, identifying details, and personal characteristics have been changed to protect the privacy and confidentiality of individuals. Any resemblance to actual persons, living or deceased, is purely coincidental and unintentional.

The content of this book reflects the author's personal experiences, perspectives, and opinions. It is not intended to diagnose, treat, or prevent any physical, psychological, or emotional condition, nor is it a substitute for professional medical or mental health advice, diagnosis, or treatment.

The author and publisher expressly disclaim any and all responsibility for any actions taken or not taken by readers based on the contents of this book. By reading this book, you acknowledge that you do so voluntarily and that you assume full responsibility for your use of the information contained herein. If you are experiencing emotional distress or a medical issue, seek immediate help from a physician or other licensed healthcare provider.

Under no circumstances shall the author or publisher be held liable for any loss, damage, or adverse consequences—direct or indirect—allegedly arising from the use or misuse of the information contained in this book.

Dedication

To my mother, who broke a generational pattern of bad
parenting and that is her legacy.

To my father, who encouraged us to reach for the stars while
holding our feet solidly on the ground.

To my children, who are my reason for everything.
May you always own your stories and experience self-love.

Acknowledgements

I would like to thank my therapist, who taught me that I am the hero of my story. I would also like to thank my siblings and friends, who lived and breathed with me through the tough spots.

Additionally, I thank my husband, who holds me up and has my back. I "both you" now and forever.

Contents

Foreword

Carol and I met as residents—she was a second-year in neurology; I was a brand-new psychiatry intern on my very first rotation. We were both new to the area—Carol had done her first year in South Dakota before transferring to Vermont, and I had just moved from Massachusetts.

Our friendship began in the hospital, and I admired her immediately. She was sharp, calm under pressure, funny, and incredibly smart—and is still one of the smartest people I know. Over the years, we've stayed close, consulted on challenging cases, and continued to share both clinical insights and life experiences.

And yet, despite all her training and knowledge, Carol fell prey to the kind of relationship that insidiously distorts your sense of reality: narcissistic abuse and the gaslighting that so often comes with it.

The central message of *We Are Alike* is that this can happen to anyone. Intelligence, education, even clinical expertise don't make us immune. What struck me most while reading this book was how Carol was able to examine her own vulnerabilities with honesty and insight. She brings her neurologist's lens to the psychological experience of being on the other side of the narcissist, explaining the trauma bond, the cycle of abuse and intermittent reinforcement, and the physiology behind PTSD in a way that is both accessible and meaningful.

As a psychiatrist who's equally fascinated by neuro-transmitters and relationships, I found myself nodding along with her story and her reflections. This may be a memoir of survival and healing, but it is also a clinical and narrative exploration of how gaslighting works—biologically, psychologically, relationally.

Carol writes as a physician, and a teacher, but she also writes with lived experience. It's a powerful combination. She weaves together personal story and medical science, making meaning out of what she endured and offering others a language to process and describe their own experiences.

I'm heartbroken that my friend went through this. That's an understatement. But this book has healing power, and that is a gift to anyone reading it.

Carol's ability to move between the personal and the clinical is what makes this book so compelling. It's not just a story of what happened. It's an account of how someone with deep clinical knowledge came to understand what she went through—and how she was able to get free.

Rosalind Gold, MD

Board certified with American Board of Psychiatry
and Neurology

Preface

We are alike. We may not look alike, sound alike, dress alike, have the same job or education, or have the same trauma, but we are all similar enough to fall victim to a narcissist. If I could fall victim to a person with narcissistic personality disorder (NPD), you can too.

You might read this book trying to figure out how we are different, and how you could avoid this, but there will ultimately be no meaningful difference. Why is there no difference that protects you? Because it is not the victim who is at fault! The common denominator is the person with NPD. They are predators! They are ruthless! They are dangerous! My predator was Glen, and he was my husband.

I am a neurologist, and as I started my journey of healing, I needed to understand what had happened to me that affected my brain and mind to this extent. As one of my tried-and-true coping mechanisms, I read everything I could find that seemed to resonate with my story. Now I am telling my story and incorporating what I have learned, to hopefully help you identify people with NPD so you can limit your exposure to them or steer clear of them all together.

Molly, Charles, Sawyer, and Hunter are my four children. Their names have been changed to protect their privacy, but the events involving them are real. This book starts long before they were born and continues to the present, in which they are now adults. As their mother, I hope and pray they will learn from my story and that their journeys will be filled with meaningful and supportive relationships.

The events described in my story will occasionally appear chaotic. This is both to demonstrate the chaos we experienced at random intervals, and to highlight how it feels to be a part of this pattern. There are errors in texted and emailed communications between me and Glen, my ex-husband who was the narcissist in my life. These are actual quotes that I left incorrect to show you how confusing communication is with a narcissist. Also to reveal that it is extremely difficult to effectively communicate with them. If you have a hard time following the texts, you are not alone!

If you have fallen victim to a narcissist, it is time to get out. It is time to end your oppression. I had a cloud hovering over my head for years, decades really. My self-esteem was so poor from the constant diatribe from my abuser, from someone who theoretically loved me, that I believed I was a bad person. If someone complimented anything I did, my inner thought was, *If you only knew me, you would know that I am not that great. That*

I am actually a bad person. That was my cloud. It followed me everywhere. It followed me to work, where I was excelling. It followed me to marathons, where I finished every time. It followed me while I watched my children, with pride, as they excelled. It was always there. I am sad for my prior self, as I didn't deserve that cloud. Nobody deserves that. My abuser had become the custodian of my self-esteem and my self-worth.

Getting out of a relationship with a person who has NPD will not be easy, but it will be worth it. Narcissists are unable to sustain long-term relationships because they don't have empathy. Empathy is the ability to understand, and be sensitive to, the feelings of others. If you don't have empathy, you can't have healthy relationships. Of course, you can stay in the relationship, which I did for so very long, but it will be laborious as you spend your time endlessly refilling his narcissistic supply tank. (I will most typically use the pronoun "his/him" throughout this book as that is the pronoun with which my abuser identified. Narcissists can be male or female.)

This entire existence is effortful and costly, but ultimately fruitless. They. Will. Not. Change! I will say this again—they cannot sustain long-term relationships!

I was a victim, and am now a survivor, of domestic abuse. It took me a long time to realize that, and even longer to admit it to myself and then out loud. Domestic abuse, boiled down, is when one person controls another. This includes physical, emotional, verbal, and financial abuse.

I am a strong-willed, educated, financially independent woman who was raised to voice my opinions and needs. It was hard to come to the realization that someone had taken control of my life. It was scary and embarrassing—even to tell my closest friends and my family. But I did eventually tell my friends and family. They helped me climb out of the abyss of despair that had become my life. It was my friends, my mother, my children, my siblings, and eventually my therapist, who guided and healed me.

My father had passed away by the time I was making the decision to divorce my husband, but he had made several comments about Glen's selfishness that I had only been partially able to let my mind acknowledge at the time. Instead, I had placed those comments in a file in my brain to be retrieved later.

My friends, family and therapist deserve credit for helping me relocate my self-worth and happiness. I give myself credit too. It took a lot of work and painful self-discovery to get where I am today. Where am I? I am genuinely happy, fulfilled, and content. I am who I was meant to be. I love myself again.

Part I

He Leaves Me

Chapter 1

Trajectory Change

I walked from window to window, watching for Shon's car to come down the gravel road to our home.

Where is he? I wondered, growing more anxious by the minute. *He should be here by now.*

I inherently knew something was wrong. I didn't know what, but something was wrong.

I walked upstairs, pacing from window to window, looking for his car.

Still no sign.

I walked back to the main floor and again went from window to window.

It was twilight now.

My husband, Shon, and I lived in an old, quaint, rented farmhouse on the plains of South Dakota. The vantage point from the house enabled me to see for a full mile in every direction.

The year was 1987, which was prior to cell phones, but I had spoken with Shon on the landline phone as he was leaving my parents' house to drive the few miles to our home. The plan was to pick me up and then meet my parents at a restaurant for supper. It was a Wednesday evening, and we only had a short period of time to eat before we had to return to our medical school studies. I was a first-year medical student and Shon was in his fourth year.

Then I saw them, the life changing, flashing red lights. I knew Shon had been in a car accident and I knew he was dead. I don't know if this was a premonition or a fear, but I knew he was dead.

I grabbed my keys, sprinted out the door, jumped in the car, and started driving toward the flashing lights, which were one mile away across the corn fields, but two miles by car.

I kept telling myself, *Drive safely! Maybe it isn't him and I need to be safe for our long life together.*

I stopped near the flashing lights, flew out of my car, ran a few steps, stopped, and looked back at my car. Crap! I had left the lights on. I paused momentarily but decided to leave them on and continue to run toward the flashing red lights.

There it was, Shon's blue Chevrolet Cavalier, driver's side down in the ditch with the bottom of the car facing me. He had been broad sided on the passenger side.

In a horrified trance, I sprinted down the steep slope of the ditch toward the car. Two highway patrol officers stopped me.

I screamed in a pleading, desperate voice, "That is my

husband's car! Where is he?"

The look on their young faces revealed the unimaginable truth. They exchanged glances, one to the other, as if they were each hoping the other would answer me.

"Is he dead?" I asked.

One patrolman cautiously answered, "I think so."

"What? I need to help him!"

I took one step forward and the two patrolmen, standing on either side of me, gently grabbed my arms.

I was twenty-two years old, with braces on my teeth and a French braid in my hair. I was wearing blue jeans and a long-sleeved T-shirt with our school mascot: a coyote, drawn in cartoon form, wearing a short, white medical student coat and a stethoscope.

I couldn't breathe. I heard someone crying, guttural wailing. The sound was coming from me! Everything seemed to move in slow motion and my hearing became muffled.

I told the officers, "Let go of me. I won't go down there."

They let go immediately but remained close by my side.

A kind, gentle, motherly woman had stopped at the crash site. She walked over to us, put her arm on my shoulder and gently led me to her open car door. Her daughter, about ten years old, sat in the back seat with wide eyes as she witnessed unbridled emotion pour out of me.

I just kept crying and crying. I was physically unable to stop. I remember my logical brain telling me to stop as it was not helping anything, but I couldn't. I felt trapped in time, like I couldn't move past that moment. Like if I moved past that moment, it was real.

This woman who wrapped me in her warmth was one of the many saviors who have come into my life, and I appreciate her so much, but I was too lost in my grief to even know what she looked like.

While my life unraveled, my parents arrived at the restaurant where Shon and I were scheduled to meet them. One of the officers asked me if he could contact my parents, then called the restaurant and informed the owner that there was an accident, and that my parents needed to come right away. I later learned that my parents did not know that Shon had been alone in the accident; they had believed that both of us had been in the deadly crash.

On seeing my parents at the accident site, I ran into my father's open arms and sobbed, "Shon's dead!"

I collapsed into his arms while my mother cried, both arms around my father and me.

As my parents held me, I thought, *Shon is dead, but we shouldn't be standing in the middle of a highway.* I find it interesting that my logical brain was trying to maintain some level of control over the situation.

My senses were overloaded with voices from the police radio, the other people from the crash walking around, and the flashing, red lights that were incessantly imprinting upon my memory. To this day, more than three decades after the crash, I have post-traumatic stress disorder (PTSD) that is activated whenever I see flashing red lights or hear sirens. I get an immediate adrenaline rush, or limbic system activation, as I know to call it now through my training as a neurologist. My four kids know to call me if they are late arriving home, because I will pace from window to window looking for flashing, red lights.

Several months later, my dad admitted that he was so relieved that I was alive, and that he had a hard time grasping the concept that Shon was dead.

I later learned that the driver of the other vehicle had been drinking alcohol. I was told that he still had the bottle with him when he arrived at the radiology department at the hospital. I know this because one of my friends who was in the medical school class one year behind me, was working in the radiology department when the driver was taken to the hospital to be checked after the motor vehicle accident.

I am not sure if he was legally drunk. I did not have the ability to care about that in my early widowhood days. I was simply just surviving_and aching for my husband.

The last thing I had told Shon was "I love you" and the last thing he had told me was "I love you too." The love of my life was gone forever. Forever.

Chapter 2

Growing Up

Sugar and spice and everything nice. Nah, although I was shy as a child I have always been made of sass, grit, and perseverance. I forgot what I was made of for a while, a couple decades really, but I eventually found myself again.

I was born into an intact, traditional family. It ultimately did not remain as such, as my parents divorced when I was twenty-seven years old. My parents have both passed away, my father in 2013 from a brain tumor and my mother in 2022 from congestive heart failure. My father was a small-town family doctor, and my mother was a stay-at-home mom and horse trainer.

I am the second of five children, with literally the best siblings in the world. We fought like crazy when we were growing up, but we have been able to move through growth, joy, and grief together, while always staying well bonded.

I have wanted to be a doctor for as long as I can remember, other than the brief times I wanted to be a ballerina and then a horse jockey. Those other dreams were less attainable, as I have no rhythm, and I am scared to ride a sprinting horse. Although not at all easy, medical school was my easiest, and safest, path.

"Dad, can I go with you?" I would beg when my father's pager would go off for after-hours emergencies.

My dad would usually relent and let me tag along. This was before healthcare privacy laws and it would never be allowed today, but I was able to see lots of coughs, chest pain, stitches, and broken bones.

Eventually I became a nurse's aide and was able to observe much more, including the delivery of babies. I even observed some surgeries.

I watched and learned as my father approached each patient with confidence. Confidence from his years of training, his extensive knowledge base, and his expertise. Patients are vulnerable when ill and they were visibly comforted by my father's presence. They treated him with great respect. I learned from my father that human life is sacred, and it is a privilege to care for patients. There is no safe shortcut, so I took the long, hard, and rewarding road to become a medical doctor, just like my father.

I have always had perseverance. If I start something, I finish it. I really don't even consider any other option.

When I was about nine years old, my maternal grandmother asked me, "What do you want to be when you grow up?"

"I want to be a doctor."

She responded, "You will never be a doctor."

"Yes, I will," I said in a matter-of-fact tone over my shoulder as I left the room.

I didn't say this to be argumentative or disrespectful. I said it because, even at that age, I knew she was not basing her response on any facts. She was not around often, so she did not know my grades, my intellect, or my drive.

My dreams were larger than she was able to envision for me, and probably for herself when she was younger. Her own mother left her when she was very young. She was raised by her father alone for a few years and then they were joined by her stepmother, whom she always disliked.

I now understand that my grandmother probably had borderline personality disorder, but I certainly couldn't put our conversation into any context as a preteen. She was just a mean person.

Her hurtful words did not deter me, but rather served as fuel for my fire. I would occasionally think of her comment during my long hours in the college library. I would remind myself, *I can do this. I will do this.*

Her comments showed me that I didn't need everyone's approval and encouragement. I could push myself. I just needed my own inner drive.

For my tenth birthday, all I wanted was a unicycle. I have no idea where this desire originated. My parents were masters at encouraging our dreams, so they bought me a unicycle.

I spent the entire summer teaching myself how to ride it. There was no YouTube to learn from, so I used the trial-and-error method.

Our neighbor, on our quiet street, hauled gasoline for a living. He had a big red truck, with a ladder up the side. This truck was parked across from our yard every evening and weekend for the entirety of my youth.

I would hang onto the ladder, get myself steadied on top of the unicycle, and let go. I would pedal until I fell. Then I would repeat the process over and over.

For the first few weeks, I could only go a few feet. Eventually, I was able to go as far as I wanted, even mastering turns. I was able to get up without the assistance of the ladder by the end of the summer as well.

At one point, about midsummer, I rode my unicycle from the road and up onto our driveway. There was a little lip or bump at the transition from the road to the driveway. My unicycle stopped short at that bump, but my body kept its forward momentum. I fell forward, hitting my chin on the bumper of Dad's parked car. It didn't hurt much, and I got up and picked up my unicycle. I felt wetness on my neck and realized that blood was running from my chin onto my neck.

I went into the house, praying I didn't need stitches. My dad looked at my wound, got up, took me to the clinic, and stitched me up.

I can still ride that same unicycle today.

That summer was the year I joined the swim team. I had been taking swim lessons for a few years, but I was not old enough to progress to my next level of Senior Life Saving, as you had to be at least sixteen years old. Since I wanted to keep swimming, I took Junior Life Saving three times. One day, after swim class, I watched the swim team start their practice.

"I want to do that," I told Mom.

My siblings and I joined and that started our era of swimming. There was no pool in our small town, so my mother, and occasionally my father, drove us forty-five minutes to another town for swim practice every weekday, with meets on the weekends. From the first practice, I loved swimming. I excelled and qualified for Nationals in the backstroke when I was sixteen.

By this time, I had learned that any sport involving a ball was not for me. I simply don't possess eye-hand coordination. But swimming came more easily, and I loved it! I even swim in my dreams. I have had the same dream for several years. If I want to get somewhere fast, I jump into the air and start "swimming." I can go as fast and as high as I want.

I am grateful for my innate need to persevere. This quality pushed me to stay in medical school after the death of my husband. When everything in my life fell apart, I needed to sustain my original dream. I needed to somehow stay me. To have some thread that kept me tethered to who I was.

I didn't go into primary care like my father but instead chose to be a neurologist. This field fits my love of organization. The brain is organized in its pathways and in its response to disease within these pathways. It also fits my fascination with understanding the human brain and my more newly-discovered fascination with the human mind.

Chapter 3

Falling in Love

College was the first step in pursuing my dream to become a medical doctor. I majored in biology with a minor in chemistry. I was very intent on single-mindedly working toward my goal. But, at the beginning of my sophomore year, I met Shon. Shon saw me in the school cafeteria and asked my best friend, Maria, if I was single, which I was. Maria was coincidentally dating Shon's best friend, Jacob.

Our first date was a double date with Maria and Jacob. We went to a couple bars in our small college town. When we left the first bar, we got to the car in the parking lot. As Shon opened the car door for me, he put his hand on my arm. A subtle, warm electric current went through me. I had never felt that, and it seemed like something important was happening.

While we were at the second bar, I got up to use the restroom. When I came back, Shon stood up and pulled out my chair for me. Jacob teased him, but Shon just smiled. He was a gentleman and was not afraid to be outwardly chivalrous. He had been raised by great parents, and he was mimicking his father's behavior.

Shon and I spent lots of time talking right from the start. He genuinely wanted to get to know me. He made me feel special and important. He was in his first year of medical school and I was busy with my undergraduate classes. Studying together became our routine. We would meet at the library after supper, study until 11 p.m. when the library closed, and then either go to his house or our respective places to continue to study for another hour or two. On the weekends, we would study from 7:30 a.m. until midnight, typically with only brief breaks for meals or a walk. Our classes were rigorous, so it worked out well that we could both get our studying done and be together.

Shon was my biggest supporter. If I had a hard test coming up, he would cheer me on and tell me I was smart.

If I thought I had done poorly, he would say, "Did you try your best?"

I would answer, "Yes."

He would raise his eyebrows, cock his head slightly to one side and say, "Well, that is all you can do, and I am sure it was enough."

He made me feel like I could accomplish anything.

His mother loves to tell the story of when Shon and I were at his parents' house a few months after we started dating. Shon was in the kitchen helping her with supper dishes when I walked through the kitchen. Shon looked at me and then smiled at his mother and said, "Isn't she beautiful?"

I always felt like I was special when I was with him.

When I would cry, Shon would kiss my tears. He told me, "If you drink someone's tears, you will be together forever."

We got engaged during my junior year of college and got married one month after my college graduation. At that time, Shon had just finished his third year of medical school.

We married on a beautiful spring day at 11 a.m., as this is my favorite time of day.

I wore a white princess dress with small, pale pink accent flowers around the waist. I was annoyed that I had gotten orthodontic braces during my freshman year, and they were not even close to coming off for the wedding. I guess when your life is easy to that point, inconsequential issues take on a bigger life than they should.

Shon wore a light gray tuxedo, with a pale yellow pocket square. He loved to wear nice things. He was tall, athletic, and lean, so he always looked elegant when he got dressed up.

At the end of the wedding ceremony, the priest had us face the crowd and he presented us to our family and friends as a married couple. The last song started, and I looked at Shon before we started the walk back down the aisle. He looked deep into my eyes with a slight smile on his lips. We held each other's gaze for several seconds. He looked so content, with pure love in his eyes. That felt so good. I have thought of that moment frequently since then. I was loved and I loved him back with my whole heart.

We went on our honeymoon to Hawaii, and it was filled with relaxation, fun, and adventure. We felt we had everything we needed, and we were excited about having the rest of our lives together.

When we returned from our honeymoon, I started my first year of medical school and he started his last. Our life was right on track. School was hard but we had each other, and we were working toward our career goals.

As I started classroom work, Shon continued with his clinical rotations. He decided that radiology was the career for him. He soon started his applications and interviews. It was fun watching his excitement grow as he stepped closer and closer to this dream.

During the fourth year of medical school, students choose the medical specialty they want to pursue—such as pediatrics, surgery, or psychiatry, to name just a few—and then begin the process of securing a residency, which is the hands-on training that follows graduation. This process is called "The Match."

Here's how it works: each medical student applies to and interviews with residency programs at hospitals across the country. Afterward, the student ranks the programs in order of preference, from most to least desired. At the same time, each residency program ranks the students who interviewed with them.

All of these rankings are entered into a national computerized system, which uses an algorithm to match students with the highest-ranked program that also ranked them highly in return. Because each residency program has a limited number of spots, students are essentially competing for placement—and the outcome can shape their entire career.

It's a high-stakes, emotionally intense process—stressful, yes, but also incredibly exciting!

Shon matched into a radiology residency in Michigan, and we were relieved and excited.

For the one birthday we shared as a married couple, Shon gave me a card that he said expressed his exact feelings. It contained a message written by Linda DuPuy Moore and it essentially said that when he was younger, he longed to meet someone who would love him completely and see him for who he truly is—someone who would understand his hopes, cheer him on, and believe in the dreams he carried. In time, that wish came true. He treasured me for loving him exactly as he once imagined.

But the dream did not continue as planned. On April 2, 1987, nine and a half months after we married, Shon died in the car accident while driving home from a medical school primary care rotation.

Shon had kissed my tears, but the legend did not hold true in the way I desired. He was not going to be with me in the tangible realm. However, the influence Shon had on my life has remained very impactful still today, more than thirty-five years after his death.

In the instant of his death, the trajectory of my life took a drastic turn.

Chapter 4

I Am a Widow

We left the accident scene—the previously nondescript site that had become a vital marker in my life journey. Going forward, my story would be explained in terms of "before the accident" and "after the accident."

I walked into our—now only my—rental home feeling disoriented and utterly overwhelmed.

My thoughts raced and swirled:

How can something so inconceivably awful be true? I can't do this. This is too hard. I will not be able to keep living without my Shon. How can the future as I knew it, just one hour ago, be gone? I grabbed Shon's blue running hoodie off the door handle where he had hung it the day prior. I brought it to my nose. I smelled him and hugged the empty jacket.

My parents guided me up the stairs to our bedroom. I realized I would never sleep in that bed with Shon again. I was suddenly alone, just half of a whole.

The realization hit me that I needed to call Shon's parents. *Oh God!* I called, but the phone was busy. I called two more times, and the phone remained busy.

My mother suggested I call their pastor, whom they were very close to. The pastor answered the phone, and I said, "Shon was in a car accident and . . . he died."

Oh my God! I said that out loud. It is real. I felt like I couldn't catch my breath. I thought, *Is this what panic feels like?*

The pastor drove to his parents' home and delivered the awful news to his mother. They called Shon's father, and he quickly headed home. He was pulled over for speeding on his drive and he told the officer, "My son just died in a car accident. I am leaving right now. Follow me home to give me a ticket if you need to." They escorted him home and then drove away.

I gathered a few things, and my parents drove me to our family home a few miles away.

As my father drove, and my mother sat in the back seat with me, I asked, "Will they make me quit school?" I don't know why I thought this, but it felt like the rug of my life had been pulled out from under my feet. Nothing seemed like a constant anymore.

My mom said, "Of course not. You will return when you are ready."

Shon's parents and fifteen-year-old twin brothers arrived at my parents' house about an hour after I got there. The boys were pale, their eyes were wide, and they appeared stunned. Their big brother was dead. We all hugged and cried together.

By this point, I was already emotionally exhausted, but I had only just begun my grief sojourn.

Through the evening, I sat with my family, Shon's family, and my close friends. It was surreal. I just kept crying. When I would get control of my emotions, someone else would lose control and I would start crying again.

By this point, I was so exhausted that I needed to sleep, yet deep sleep eluded me. I would sleep briefly, awaken, realize it was true, and be hit with the full assault of grief all over again. I started to dread falling asleep.

Even though it is figurative rather than literal, heartbreak feels physical when it is raw and horrendous. In those first days, weeks and even months, I felt an ache and heaviness in the middle of my chest that was beyond anyone's reach to lessen my intense grief. Heartbreak made me draw my arms toward my center in a futile attempt to prevent my fragile being from shattering further. In an attempt to prevent me from dying of grief.

My heartbreak permeated through me and settled in my soul. It became part of my DNA. An inextricable part of me.

I couldn't eat anything Shon liked. I couldn't eat anything Shon hated. I couldn't eat much of anything, except fruit. I would swallow, but the grief would bubble up and make it hard to eat more.

I went to the funeral home with my parents the next day. There he was, looking like he was asleep. I felt so much better when I was with him. I was so very sad, but all I wanted was Shon. I needed him. I needed to be with him! Even in death, I was comforted by him.

There I was, twenty-two years old, picking out a casket for my beautiful twenty-six-year-old husband. The cacophony in my head was a banter of, *Do I get a nice one? Do I get the cheaper one? Does it matter? What would Shon want?* Impossible! Impossible decisions that needed to be made quickly. I picked the middle price because I was simply unable to use my brain to make this decision. Honestly, there is a little blurring of some of these memories as I was barely functioning at that point.

There are certain slap-in-the-face reality checks that happen after the death of a loved one. For me, one of those moments was the process of picking out clothes for Shon to be buried in. I looked in his closet and tried to decide what he would want to wear for eternity. I found myself pondering the pair of pants that he loved but were a little itchy . . . nope, not those. *And what shoes? Does he wear shoes in the casket? What about a tie? I don't want them to make it too tight. He hates that!* I chose a pair of gray pants with a classic blue blazer and red tie. I closed the closet door and walked away. One decision down, an endless number of impossible decisions to go.

Next on the list of unimaginable tasks was choosing the cemetery and plot. His parents took this off my plate, which I was very thankful for. They chose a beautiful spot with rolling hills and old trees. Next decision, one plot for him alone or two side-by-side plots for both of us? I pride myself in my quick decision-making skills, but I was unable to make this decision. I wanted to be with Shon for all eternity, but I was twenty-two and would likely marry again and have a family. *How do I discuss this with his mother, who was also grieving?* Fortunately, I didn't have to. Without prompting, his mother said, "I know you will get married again someday, but for now we will plan on you being together." What a beautiful gift!

We have plots together and the headstone bears both our names.

The visitation was held, and I didn't know what I was supposed to do. I had not had any close family or friends die up to that point in my young life. I pulled a chair over to the casket and sat next to Shon, holding his cold hand and memorizing his face. People came and went all day. It was physically and emotionally exhausting.

My grandfather, a stoic farmer, came in and started crying. I recall thinking, *This is so bad that even Grandpa is crying.* So I cried again.

Jacob came in, caught sight of Shon, and lost all control. He started sobbing and ran out of the building. Maria looked at me, totally torn as to whom she should comfort first. Her face looked so sad. Someone came over by me and she took that opportunity to find her husband. She found him squatting down, with his head in his hands and his back against the building. He was devastated!

The time for the funeral arrived. I was dreading this part of the process and was honestly ready to get this over with. We all met at Shon's parents' house so we could go to the funeral together. When it was time to leave for the ceremony, I went to my dad's car and stood by the door. I stood there for several seconds, not making a move to open the door. Shon had always opened my car door, and it didn't even cross my mind to do it myself. My brother, Mark, realized what was happening as I stood there frozen. He came over and opened the door for me and I got in. That was another slap-in-the-face moment. My life had changed.

As we drove to the funeral on a beautiful April day, I was stunned that life was going on as normal for the rest of the world. There were people out walking and some boys were playing basketball. I wondered how something this devastating was not immobilizing everyone. How was life moving forward? How had I been left behind?

I walked up the church aisle in my black dress with my parents on either side of me holding me up and guiding me forward to the front pew. I felt like I was living someone else's life. How could I be walking up an aisle with my parents in a black dress when I had done that a few months previous in a white dress?

Tears literally streamed down my face for the whole service. Shon's church choir sang "On Eagle's Wings" by Father Michael Joncas. That song is so beautiful, but ever since the funeral, it induces intense sadness deep within my soul. This occurs so rapidly that I rarely have a chance to remind myself that I am no longer in that moment.

Out of intense love, Shon's father summoned the courage to deliver his first-born child's eulogy. Now that I have my own children, I am even more in awe that he had the strength and composure to do this. It was a heartfelt speech filled with gratitude for the privilege of parenting Shon, sadness for his lost child, and the potential he had to help others and the acknowledgment of the grief in all our hearts. We walked out, bore the seemingly unending receiving line in which I continued the endless stream of tears. We left and that was that.

Now came the next step—living my life alone. Shon was gone and friends and family eventually returned to their own lives. They were always there for me of course, but I was the one left to deal with it at the end of the day. This was my cross to bear.

Chapter 5

Grief

Dr. Elisabeth Kubler-Ross, a Swiss psychiatrist, developed a model that describes five stages of grief. The stages include denial, anger, bargaining, depression, and acceptance. These do not necessarily occur in order and getting through one and moving to the next does not mean you are done with the prior stages. You vacillate forward and back and then forward again.

The denial for me was immediate. It was just so hard to fathom that something so awful could actually be true.

As I have previously explained, I had a hard time allowing myself to fall asleep because I knew I would awaken with the immediate realization that this was real. I would think, "Oh my God, Shon is dead! This can't be. This is too much. I cannot live."

I don't know when that stopped, but it eventually did and reality took up residence in my soul.

Anger hit hard.

Even in church. When I went to church the Sunday after Shon's funeral, the mass was the story of how three people were raised from the dead by Jesus. This made me so angry.

I wanted to yell at the priest, *Tell him to bring Shon back! Shon was good! I need him!*

Additionally, I had a hard time making it through the service because by this time people knew this tragedy had occurred. I was now the 22-year-old widow. That was the trait I would be identified by for several years.

People would look at me but not know what to say, so they would look away.

I just needed to get away from there.

A few days later, I walked down to the pond on our family farm. It was a rare moment that I was alone, as my family was still staying close by my side.

I walked toward the pond on this pretty spring day. I crossed the plowed corn field, shimmied between the rows of barbed wire fence, and walked to the small, muddy beach area. I stood there awhile and tried to make some sense of this life. I then walked to the tree where Shon and I had taken pictures a few months prior. I was suddenly overcome with sorrow and pure rage. I picked up a large branch and repeatedly hit it against the tree, until it broke in two. I fell onto my knees in the grass, sobbing until I seemed to have no more tears to cry.

I was so damn angry that Shon was taken from me. *Why him? Why me?*

Bargaining was brief for me from what I recall. Actually, I don't know if I technically went through this stage as I had nothing to bargain for. He was suddenly dead from the trauma. I could not bargain that I would pray more if he could just survive, or that I would be mentally fine even if he were quadriplegic but alive. I use quadriplegia as an example because his neck was broken in the accident.

Maybe it was bargaining when I wanted one more day with Shon. I realized quickly that a day would never be enough and when that day was over, my grief would start fresh again.

I did want a redo of the moments just prior to his death, so maybe that was my bargaining. Since I had spoken to him just before he got in the car, I thought about how my life would be if I had talked for one minute less or one minute more. He then would not have been hit by that car. I think I would call this stage more of a guilt situation than bargaining. I felt guilty for the wrong amount of time in which I had kept him on the phone.

I am not sure how grief could happen without depression. They are inextricably linked. I was so sad and felt so lost and empty.

In retrospect, I was undoubtedly clinically depressed. I had a hard time concentrating in school. Memorizing has always been relatively easy for me, but I could not do it. My mind would not stay focused long enough to form a pathway for new material in my brain.

As a result, I hobbled through my second year of medical school.

I then spread my last two years of school over a three-year period. That gave me more time to learn and more time to attempt to heal.

I did not get therapy, nor was it suggested by my loved ones or the psychiatrist I was with almost daily for nine weeks in a medical school rotation.

I definitely needed it!

I am not sure why this was not recommended. I think mental health and its treatment were considered taboo in that era. I, myself, did not seek it out as I thought I would not get into a residency program if I had a perceived big black mark in my history. That was so dumb! They would have understood.

I wish I had gotten therapy. The trauma was just too big for me to navigate alone.

The fifth stage of grief is acceptance. My mind is black and white enough to have accepted the reality that Shon was dead shortly after the immediate shock wore off. However, without therapy, I did not accept the implications of that loss. The main implication being that I no longer had the person who loved me unconditionally, for just being me. In my immature, traumatized brain, I wanted to believe that feeling could be replaced by just any human. I simply needed to find my next love, and I would be back on track. Then, when I found something that initially felt similar, my single-minded focus allowed me to ignore warning signs and walk into the waiting arms of a narcissist. I was the perfect, vulnerable prey for the predator.

I recall a sudden crushing sense of finality six months after the accident. At that point, your loved ones have gotten back to their own lives and the reality of forever has sunken in. So, acceptance? I didn't want to accept it, but I knew at that moment that this was final. There was nothing anyone could do about it. So, there it was, I guess. Acceptance stage completed.

Did Shon go through these stages in heaven? Did he want to come back to me and his family? Did he want to come back and walk through his graduation ceremony two weeks after his death? I did this. I walked though his medical school graduation, in his place. His classmates requested this, and I was grateful they wanted Shon to be part of the ceremony.

Two weeks after Shon's death, I lined up with his classmates behind the bleachers, his closest friends staying by my side. We walked toward the rows of chairs, as proud family members sat in the stadium seats. I sat in Shon's assigned spot and waited for his name to be called. I walked across the stage as if in a dream state and received his diploma. It should have been such a happy day, and it was unbearably sad. It made me feel nauseous. There was huge applause as Shon's name was called. Shon's parents and my parents were in the stands, as we were all attempting to support each other.

After I received the diploma, I walked between curtains to the back of the stage. I could not make myself walk back to the chair and sit down. I could not take it anymore. My angel stood just behind the curtains in the form of my medical school classmate. She was there for a family member of hers that was graduating, but she was certainly placed in my path by God. I needed her desperately. She opened her arms, and I collapsed into them. She held me until my parents and Shon's parents gathered me up, again.

Chapter 6

Letters to Shon

While learning to deal with unfamiliar and intense emotions, I started a new journal in which I wrote letters to Shon. This was my first introduction to journaling, other than the brief inserts into my diary in elementary school in which I quickly realized nothing exciting was happening by that point in my life. I did, however, lock it up with the little, golden key, just in case my siblings decided to peek at my deep feelings about how I "got up, ate breakfast, and watched cartoons."

My first letter to Shon was eleven days after his death, on April 13, 1987. It is hard for me to read, even now. It displays the raw emotion of an overwhelmed, devastated, and traumatized young widow.

Dear Shon,

Do you remember when we used to talk about how much we would miss each other if the other one died? Well, it's at least as bad as we imagined. I miss you so much that I just feel my heart will split in two.

I miss your smile, your arms, your kisses, your confidence . . . but, most of all, I miss that special look in your eyes that required no explanation (as described in our favorite Carole King song, "Life Without Love") and told me just how much you loved me. I quite often wonder how I will live forever without that.

It hurts so bad to see and smell your clothes and know I'll never see you in them again. Everything hurts so bad Shon.

Dad and I went to our house to get some things. I was so lonesome for you I felt sick all over on the inside. Everywhere I looked I could see you and I doing something.

Oh Shon, I love you so much! I really don't know how I will ever manage without you. I loved how our life was working, I loved it, and I didn't want to give it up. My life seems like such a turmoil now, and you, more than anyone, know how much I hate that.

I hope you're happy in heaven. I think one of the only things that has kept me going this long, is to remember that you are here with me, in a different form than I would like, but none-the-less, with me. I like to feel that you are still watching over and protecting me.

Remember that someday we will be together again,

you, me and Kihei (our dog that died in the accident with Shon). Wait for me, okay.

Love,
Your wife, Carol

April 14, 1987:

Dear Shon,

Things are so-so down here. Sometimes I really feel like I can adjust to my new life; other times I feel like it's impossible. I know that whether I adjust to you being gone or not, you're still not coming back, so I guess I have no choice but to suck it up and move forward.

Sometimes when I feel like I can make it, I feel guilty. Partly because I have to sometimes consciously try to forget you and how perfect you were, in order for the pain to subside.

I went for a walk around the pond tonight. I cried and cried because I miss you so bad, also because it's still hard to believe and accept that you're dead, and also because I am really scared. I'm scared to live without you, I'm scared about school and how I'll handle it without my number one supporter, and I'm scared of all the different things that keep going through my mind that I just can't find answers to.

I'm going to go to sleep . . . stay with me though.

Love always,
Your wife, CB

May 5, 1987:

Dear Shon,

I have missed you awfully bad today. Sometimes the pain is overwhelming, and I feel if it gets even a tiny bit worse, I'll go crazy.

Do you remember our kiss the night before you died? I was laying on the couch and you were sitting on the floor. It was a beautiful, loving kiss and I will remember and cherish it forever just as I will our last kiss before you left that dreaded morning.

Love you now and always,
Your wife, CB

May 25, 1987:

Dear Shon,

Sometimes I scare myself because it still hits so hard when I remember you have died. I mean, I know it's true, but every once in a while, I think about it, and it hurts as if I just found out.

I went to your grave three times today. Sometimes, when I miss you so bad, it helps to be near you.

Love,
Your lonesome wife, CB

May 27, 1987:

Dear Shon,

I'm really scared for June 14 (our first wedding anniversary). I would have never imagined I'd visit my husband's grave on our first anniversary. It sucks! The whole deal sucks!

Love you now and forever,
Your wife, CB

June 9, 1987:

Dear Shon,

I'm finally done with this semester. It's really a relief to be able to put studying behind me for a while.

Now that school is over for the year, I have more time to think. That scares me and a lot of times I stop myself from thinking about you because I don't want the hurt to come. I know I need to work through all my feelings, but it scares me so much, I have to turn it off sometimes. I don't want to do this too often because I don't want to repress my grief and then go crazy later because I haven't worked through it.

I really miss you bad Shon. I keep thinking through my worst two memories . . . when I asked if you were dead and they said, "I think so," and the first time I saw you after the accident. These two memories seem to hurt the worst.

I'm going to sleep. Hopefully my dreams will be filled with memories of you.

Love,
CB

November 4, 1987

Dear Shon,

I think I'm doing pretty well overall, Shon. I think you would be proud of me. "I am doing my best and that is all that matters." It still hurts really bad. Sometimes when I just sit and think, the full and total reality that this is forever overwhelms me. I will never see you again . . . until I'm in heaven. That whole concept is hard to understand and accept.

I have been considering deferring school for one year. I really want to keep going but it just seems too hard. When I think ahead, I think of Christmas, the anniversary of your death, finals, boards, and our second anniversary. It all seems impossible to handle. I just have to keep remembering that what I want is at the end of all my hard work, and that I can do it. Plus, there is the pool that I dream of some day. I know you would be telling me I can do it, so that is what I am going to try to do.

I'd better get some sleep. Please stay with me and help me through the rough spots.

Love forever and ever,
CB

April 16, 1988

Dear Shon,

I made it through the dreaded one-year anniversary of your death. I survived, mostly by keeping busy and trying to ignore it. I have also made it through another set of final exams. I am now starting my preceptorship and will start studying for boards soon. I have had a hard time concentrating since you died, so I hope that returns to normal soon.

Please help me with this whole Glen business. It is so confusing. He acts like he likes me when we're together, but then he will wait a long time before calling me for another date. I hate the stupid games. You spoiled me with your openness. I hate trying to guess what is going on in his head! I hate that I had to enter the dating scene again.

Love always,
CB

Wow! This was interesting for me to read as I was writing this book. If only I had the capacity at that time to listen to my inner voice. My gut was telling me something about Glen, but I was so desperate to love again that I was unable to listen.

Chapter 7

My Sister's Journal

When my mother died, my younger sister, Amelia, and I were cleaning out her storage unit. We found some random pages of Amelia's journal that had fallen out of a box. The pages displayed her own letters to Shon. Neither of us knew the other was writing these letters. She was sixteen years old when he died, and he was very special to her.

Shon and I went to as many of her track meets and basketball games as we could. Amelia was a high jumper, and Shon had done that during his high school days as well. During track meets, Amelia would come over to Shon after each jump for advice. Then she just kept jumping higher and higher.

Here is an excerpt from her diary:

Right now, I am thinking about Shon, so I decided to start this diary because I can't seem to talk to anyone about how I feel and maybe it will help to write it down.

> *Dear Shon,*
>
> *I miss you so much. I think of you whenever I play basketball or go running or do anything with Carol. Who is going to be around to help me with all my sports next year and give me advice and help? I miss you a lot and I can just imagine how much Carol must miss you. You were so great all the time, ever since I met you, I liked you. I'm sorry that I haven't come to visit you at the cemetery.*
>
> *I love you and miss you terribly.*
> *I miss you, Shon!*

She followed this with a letter to God. The stages of grief are apparent in her letter, as she was angry and bargaining.

> *Dear God,*
>
> *I hope you can understand why I don't like to go to church anymore but I just can't get myself to go to worship you when a lot of the things you let happen are so unfair. Shon could have done so much for all the people down here. My faith is really weak right now but I'm trying to work it out.*
>
> *What have we done to deserve this? You could have fixed this so it didn't happen.*

She did eventually regain her faith, but you can definitely feel her pain, anguish, and struggle in these letters.

Chapter 8

Moving On

After Shon died, I could not stay at the house we shared for even one night. When I was there, I felt a suffocating and crushing sorrow deep within my soul. How would I go on? I didn't know and could not fathom it in those early days.

I was also uncomfortable in our home, as we had experienced a break-in about one week before Shon died. Fortunately, Shon and I had both gotten home at the same time. We walked to our back door and saw that it was wide open. As we got closer, we could tell the door had been kicked in. Pieces of the door frame littered the steps leading to the basement. We went in and examined each room together. Fortunately, we didn't find anyone there and it did not appear that anything had been stolen. In retrospect, I am not sure why it didn't cross our minds to call the police, but we didn't. After Shon died, I was worried this person would return.

So I moved back to my childhood home while I finished the last weeks of my first year of medical school. About one week after the funeral, my maternal grandmother came to visit. When she came up to my room and sat on the bed beside me, her psychopathology was on full display. She had suffered the tragic loss of her nine-year-old son decades prior, when he was hit by a car while riding his bike.

Now, she declared to me, "The death of a child is much worse than the death of a spouse. When you lose a child, you lose a part of you."

Well, so much for sage advice from my elder, I guess.

I recall being totally perplexed by this obnoxious comment, but I didn't have the energy to do anything but continue to listen as she droned on and then left my room.

Of course, I agree the death of a child is horrible beyond belief. I have watched Shon's parents struggle with their loss for years. However, telling a new twenty-two-year-old widow that her grieving is not as valid as hers is shameful. It is not a competition; they are both earth-shattering!

Later, I moved into an apartment that was close to my parents' house. I was so lonely there without Shon. This was not the plan I wanted. The hideous, grass green carpet throughout the apartment put a big exclamation point on the tragedy of my situation. It was actually comical if it weren't so sad.

The apartment complex consisted of eight apartments, all occupied by widowed women in their eighties. I joined them as an outlier based upon my age alone.

I took just one week off from school before returning to take my final exams. Those went well, probably because that information had already been stored in my brain before the accident. I then had two months off for summer break before starting my second year. My decision to return to school so quickly was based on one fact. I simply couldn't fathom losing anything else in my life.

In retrospect, I definitely should have taken a year off to grieve. I was so young and so traumatized. My brain was just slower, making it so much harder to learn new information compared to the prior year. I wish a loved one would have suggested that I take a year off, but they were also grieving, and they needed me to be okay, or at least appear to be okay. Had I taken the time to grieve, would I have fallen for a narcissist? I honestly don't know.

I was definitely loved and protected by many during the next few years. Several times during my year in this apartment, I would come home after an evening of studying to find a plate of homemade cookies in the hall outside my door. Almost nightly, I would pull into the parking lot and see a light go out in one specific unit. I had a guardian angel watching out for me and making sure I made it home. She understood.

Chapter 9

Gone

I knew Shon for a total of four years. Four years! It was such a small amount of time when you consider the span of my lifetime. It was a short percentage of my life, yet he made a profound impact that has persisted to this day. He showed me how to love and be loved. He showed me that perseverance leads to results. He showed me that you can be confident without being cocky.

But he is gone. Gone from my physical world but not gone from my heart and soul. I think of him often, but with fondness rather than sadness. I see him in my dreams. I can remember the look in his eyes when he looked into mine. I can recall very vivid memories, but I can't recall the sound of his voice. That remains unreachable.

I needed to move forward with my life, so I did. The next part of my story was supposed to be good, but it was not. The following pages outline how my life went from sad to a different variation of sad.

Part II

I Leave Him

Chapter 10

Trapped

My second husband, Glen, satanically grinned at me as he rearranged the elliptical exercise machine to face away from the TV where my movie was on pause.

This was a few weeks after I filed for divorce, so Glen was particularly agitated and spiteful.

He proclaimed, "Everyone knows the elliptical should face north. It has to back up to the couch in case someone falls off."

I responded, "How would you fall off the back of an elliptical? That doesn't make any sense!"

I was so sick of his nonsense! My fight or flight response triggered and then fully engaged. I picked up the front of the heavy elliptical to swing it back to face toward the TV. Glen hopped onto the elliptical, grin still in place.

In my adrenaline-induced state, I maintained my grip and moved the full weight of the machine and Glen into the position I wanted.

Our size difference was immense. Glen was six-foot, two-inches tall and 230 pounds to my five-foot, six-inches and 109 pounds. I had lost weight, which is typical for me during intensely stressful times. This was not as low as the 104 pounds after Shon's death, but certainly too light for my height. I simply had no appetite, and my metabolism was in high gear from the stress.

When I set the elliptical down, Glen was glaring at me from his perch. He twirled his index finger around his ear and mouthed, "You're crazy."

"This is my area!" I yelled. "You have claimed the main floor and upstairs! Just leave me alone down here!"

My elderly mother was with me, also waiting to watch the movie that remained frozen on the TV screen. She stood watching this unfold, in an uncharacteristically calm manner. Her arms were crossed, and she had an impassive expression on her face.

Glen turned to Mom and said, "Carol is crazy and has rage issues. I don't know what is causing her to act like this."

She did not respond to him but maintained her protective stance near me.

I tumbled into a deep abyss of acute despair. I simply couldn't take it anymore. My limbic system continued to fire, and I felt pure rage toward my abuser.

"Leave me alone!" I screamed. "I hate you and I can't stand to be around you anymore!"

This was not "rage issues" as Glen always accused me of. This was rightful anger in reaction to a stimulus. This was my frustration that Glen labeled as rage so he could tell me what a horrible person I was. I had been pushed and pushed and pushed and eventually I didn't want to be pushed any more. I had suppressed my needs and wants and feelings for years. I couldn't suppress them anymore.

This is an example of gaslighting, and I had endured this severe form of emotional abuse for years. I didn't have the term for it initially, but that is what it was. I was given the name, gaslighting, by a friend after I filed for divorce. Learning this word was life-altering.

Narcissists use gaslighting as a form of psychological manipulation where they make you doubt your own memory, perception, or sanity so they can gain control or avoid account- ability. They may deny things they said or did, twist facts, or accuse you of being "too sensitive" to make you question your reality and become dependent on their version of the truth.

As I read about what this meant, I thought, *I am not crazy like Glen says. This has a name, and this is exactly what he is doing to me.* For years, I was embarrassed by this incident as my children were upstairs and certainly heard me yelling. Through a lot of work with my therapist, I now know this was not a moment of loss of control, but rather a regaining of control. I was remem- bering that I am strong, both emotionally and physically. I was subconsciously revealing, to myself and Glen, that I was strong enough to do everything myself, and leave.

Glen was just a heavy weight that I was able to carry, but was no longer willing to carry. So, I set him down. This is what I revealed to my children. They witnessed a strong woman regaining control of her life. I modeled the setting of healthy boundaries.

Chapter 11

My Next Chapter

This section is hard for me to write for several reasons. This man was, and still is, a huge disappointment and I am embarrassed for my connection with him. Also, the bad memories far outweigh the good, so it is hard for me to find good memories to share. Honestly, I don't have many fond memories of my time with him other than those that revolve around our children.

Glen and I met when I was near the end of my second year of medical school, just over one year from when Shon died.

Glen told me he was working toward his bachelor's degree in "secondary education with a coaching certificate."

He took the classes to obtain this education degree but did not do the student teaching, so he was never able to teach.

I never saw a coaching certificate and honestly don't even know if this is a real thing. The coaching was for sports, but he never explained this more specifically. I guess I didn't question it because at that time I did not know he could lie so easily and ubiquitously.

Anyway, he never coached sports either, including even our children's little league teams when they were looking for volunteers.

Inability to complete things is part of his persona and a common trait of people with NPD.

Our relationship began in a bar in our small college town. I was out with classmates, celebrating the completion of an exam. Glen was the bartender and he was very ruggedly handsome in those years. Encouraged by my friends, I worked up the nerve to ask him for a date.

I noted early on that our dating experience was different from when I dated Shon, as noted in my diary. With Glen, everything was just harder. I recall once, he was following me by car to my apartment. He didn't know where I lived and this was before cell phones, so he was following me. When we were on a highway, I realized he was no longer in sight behind me. Of course, my PTSD symptoms started right away. I thought he had crashed. I turned my car around and retraced my path about a mile back before I saw his car parked in an approach to a field. I pulled up and asked him why he stopped.

He said, "I wanted to watch that bird."

I thought this was odd behavior. When you are following someone to an unknown location it seems like common sense to at least try to stay within sight.

When I started driving again, I wondered, *Is he that passionate about birds or is he totally invested in his own immediate desires?*

That was a small red flag that I wish, in retrospect, I had paid more attention to.

That bird was a hawk for crying out loud! It wasn't even a rare bird in this area.

Our dating started slowly. He would take me on a date, then wait a few weeks to ask me out again. I would be just about ready to give up when he would call again. In retrospect, I believe this was about control for him. Keep me on the line and reel me in at his whim. He was showing me that he was the boss of this relationship.

Eventually, we started to date regularly. As is typical with a new relationship, there was the excitement of getting to know one another and the joy of having undivided attention.

He showered me with adoration and affection. I liked that feeling. I desired that feeling. I craved that feeling. I missed that feeling. I needed that feeling.

Eventually, once you are hooked, the love-bombing stops. They love you and then they don't.

I would later learn that love-bombing is one of a narcissist's most powerful weapons. It's a form of emotional manipulation where they overwhelm you with excessive affection, praise, attention, and gifts early in a relationship to gain control, trust, or dependency. After the target becomes emotionally invested, the narcissist often shifts to criticism, manipulation, or withdrawal, creating a toxic cycle of confusion and control.

After about a year, he asked me to marry him. I said yes and thought, *Okay, my life is back on track.* Back on track for me, in my then emotionally immature brain, meant I would be back to the point I was just before Shon was torn from me. I wanted that feeling back so bad. So bad that I ignored the voice in my head that said something was just not right. I simply didn't feel the same as I had when Shon proposed.

I rationalized that I had probably idealized my relationship with Shon, making it impossible for anyone to live up to those standards.

Had I set the bar too high with Shon, or was I lowering the bar for Glen?

After one year of marriage, we moved to Vermont for my three-year neurology residency program.

I recall that things were going okay, but by that time I had realized that things needed to go the way Glen wanted. This is a relatively silly thing, but he insisted he have the small ensuite half bathroom and that I have the bathroom down the hall. Okay, whatever.

But I soon learned that his shaving ritual was obnoxiously loud. He would tap his metal shaver on the side of the porcelain sink to get the hair out from between the blades. While this is okay in and of itself, it was very loud when I would be trying to sleep after a twenty-four- or thirty-six-hour call shift. My suggestion that he shave in the other bathroom went unheeded. I just counted down the minutes before he would be done with this so I could fall back asleep.

During my last year of residency, I gave birth to Molly. I loved her at first sight and knew I would do anything to care for and protect her. But as my bond with her intensified, my relationship with Glen inversely became more strained. Glen became more self-centered and seemed to only communicate with me by commanding or by yelling.

I thought this difficulty was because my attention was appropriately focused on our newborn and from my crazy schedule as a chief resident.

The issue was not with me or Molly, though. The issue was that Glen was now witnessing the true, unwavering love that a good mother has for her child. Glen was raised by a mother that was not naturally nurturing or particularly warm. She was more of a utilitarian in how she ran her household. Glen was also the sixth of eight children. He was just another peg on the board for this family. His father was an alcoholic, which compounded the family dynamic.

I now find it interesting that I inherently blamed myself for Glen's evolving harsh behavior toward me. I have learned a lot since those years! This was a Glen issue.

His behavior insidiously changed over the next several years and continued to evolve through the decades. I was caught in his vortex of insanity. It was several years later, however, that I started to suspect narcissistic personality disorder.

Labeling Glen with NPD is purely my opinion. This opinion is substantiated by my training as a neurologist and by the knowledge I gained on my journey toward healing.

Chapter 12

What is a Neurologist?

Becoming a neurologist takes several steps and then several more. After obtaining my undergraduate degree and taking the Medical Collage Acceptance Test (MCAT), I was accepted into medical school.

My first two years of medical school were primarily classroom work designed to sturdy the science foundation upon which I would add my clinical knowledge. These two years were followed by the dreaded national medical board exam, part one. We literally had the fear of the difficulty of this exam placed in us on day one of classes. Failing this exam would mean that my dream was done. Six years of education down the drain.

My next two years consisted of 6,000 clinical hours learning my craft from physicians in different specialties. In those hours, I found my passion for neurology and decided to pursue that as my specialty.

After the classroom work and clinical hours were complete and having passed part one and part two of my boards, I was able to graduate with my Doctor of Medicine degree. I was now officially a doctor, but I still had a few years to go before I would be a master of the subject matter which would culminate in the privilege of patients placing their lives in my hands.

Next up was my intern year that involved supervised training in internal medicine. I learned about a broad range of medical conditions that I would potentially encounter while treating patients with neurologic disease. At the end of this year, I took part three of my board exams.

Neurology residency was arduous as I spent three years learning directly from neurologists in the clinic and hospital. There is now an eighty-hour work week restriction for residents. However, that restriction was not in place when I trained and I did more than a few 110-hour weeks. By the end of residency, I had completed an additional 15,000 clinical hours with a gradual increment in my level of independence.

As there is some cross-over between neurologic and psychiatric disease, I completed one month of a mandatory psychiatry rotation during my residency years.

The final step finally arrived, but it was no small hurdle. I had to pass a written and practical exam to become board certified with the American Board of Psychiatry and Neurology. The written exam was thirty-three percent psychiatry, which I had to pass separately from the neurology portion. Therefore, a strong neurology score could not carry me through the psychiatry portion. I had to have a solid grasp of both topics.

I passed and I felt Shon smiling down on me with pride. I persevered and I did it! I passed four written board exams and one practical exam, finished medical school, and completed residency. And I was proud of myself as well.

To review my psychiatry total, I had a nine-week rotation in my third year of medical school, a five-week elective in my fourth year of medical school, and four weeks in residency. Additionally, I passed the psychiatry portion of my specialty boards. So, I am indeed qualified to have an opinion on NPD.

I started my grown-up job at age thirty. As a general neurologist, I diagnose and treat anything that involves the nervous system. Diseases in my realm are many, but include such things as headache (my favorite), epilepsy, Parkinson's disease, dementia, Lou Gehrig's disease (amyotrophic lateral sclerosis or ALS), stroke, and neuropathy.

I currently work in the clinic seeing patients with neurologic symptoms. For most of my career, I also spent time in the hospital being "on call." These days were long and unpredictable as I never knew when I would be consulted on a hospital patient or called to the emergency department to see a patient there. For weekend "on call" days, I additionally rounded on my partners' patients who were still in the hospital from their call days. Call days were twenty-four to forty-eight hours long and sleep was often elusive.

Being a neurologist is very rewarding. I love putting the puzzle pieces together to make a diagnosis and treatment plan. When patients return for follow up and are better, that is icing on the cake!

Chapter 13

What is Narcissistic Personality Disorder?

As a coping mechanism, I read. The more I read, the more I learned. The more I learned, the more I journaled.

I read voraciously as this information was literally setting me free. I journaled obsessively to keep track of these enlightening insights.

I have always enjoyed losing myself in books, starting with *Black Beauty* and *Little House on the Prairie*, but this time I was finding myself. This was not a flaw in my psyche; it was a flaw in Glen's.

I was learning that it would be hard, but I could get out of this soul-sucking relationship.

I felt like I was diving into a beautiful sea of knowledge that was describing exactly what I was experiencing and giving me a way out. I was not alone! It was validating to read that other people had experienced the same confusing interactions that had consumed my life with a narcissist.

The meaning of the term narcissist has roots in Greek mythology. Narcissus was a handsome, mortal son of Gods. He loved no one, until he saw a reflection of himself in a pool of water and fell in love with his own image. He was unable to obtain the object of his desire in the water and died from his sorrow. He was replaced with a flower, also called Narcissus. There are several slight variations on this story, but in them all, Narcissus represents extreme self-adoration, rather than healthy self-love.

Narcissistic Personality Disorder (NPD), per the DSM-5 (*Diagnostic and Statistical Manual of Mental Disorders*[1], fifth edition), is a personality disorder comprising a pervasive pattern of grandiosity, a constant need for admiration, and a lack of empathy. This begins in early adulthood and tends to worsen over time. The diagnosis is made by the presence of at least five of the following criteria:

1. A grandiose sense of self-importance. They tend to exaggerate their achievements and talents. They expect to be recognized as superior with their achievements.

2. A preoccupation with fantasies of unlimited success, power, brilliance, beauty, or ideal love.

3. A belief that he or she is special and unique and can only be understood by, or should associate with, other special or high-status people or institutions.

4. A need for excessive admiration.

5. A sense of entitlement.

6. Interpersonally exploitative behavior. They take advantage of others to achieve their own needs and desires.

7. A lack of empathy. They are unwilling to recognize or identify with the feelings or needs of others.

8. Envy of others or a belief that others are envious of him or her.

9. A demonstration of arrogant and haughty behaviors or attitudes.

In addition to the clinical syndrome noted above, people with NPD are quintessentially charming and exciting. This is how the hook is set in the early stages of the relationship.

People with NPD don't have insight into their personality flaws, so they are unable to change and certainly do not take responsibility for their flaws. This is one of the reasons they are unable to sustain long-term relationships. They view themselves as perpetually blameless, and over time, the victim finds it easier to shoulder the blame than to endure yet another exhausting, circular conversation that always ends in the same untenable conclusion.

Narcissists do not function in reality, and their communication skills are atrocious. They decide to do something for their own benefit and then make up a vague and convoluted reason for why they do it. Their rationale only makes sense to them. As you try to get them to explain what they mean, they talk in circles and tangents. Somehow the topic morphs into something else, or into multiple other topics, until the victim can't tell what the person with NPD is even talking about.They constantly move the foundation on which you are trying to stand. Either no decision is made, or the abuser will insist you collaboratively came up with their conclusion. This type of communication is a manipulation tool the person with NPD uses to control you and get what they want. It was probably the most frustrating thing I encountered in dealing with my abuser.

Early in our marriage, I would try to explain the falsity of the cognitive distortion my husband had concocted. It didn't work. Not even once! It is best to just stop talking to them, because your logic—actual logic—will not get through to them.

NPD is a high-conflict personality, because they are entitled, overreactive, and unable to compromise. Additionally, they thrive on conflict. They enjoy hooking you into an argument. To make matters worse for you, their range of behaviors narrows under stress. Their emotional reactions are haphazard and therefore totally unpredictable. They are like a tired, hungry two-year-old who is easily tipped into a temper tantrum. They overreact when a desired item or response is not immediately obtained. They treat everything as a crisis and will want you to respond to their desires instantly.

Do not let the NPD pull you into their crisis mode. Pull yourself from the situation, calm yourself, and then think logically on your own timeframe. It is rarely an actual crisis, but they want you to make a rash decision, their decision. When my abuser didn't immediately get what he wanted, he would lash out verbally. He would become irrational and loudly berate his target. This was most commonly me, but it could also be our children. I couldn't stand to watch this happen to my children, so I would put myself in the path of his criticism. I would physically get into his line of view, or I would make a statement in support of my child. He would then zero his laser in on me as the new target.

When the children got older, they learned this as well. If the abuser was verbally attacking me, one of my children would step between us and take some of the heat while slowly walking toward their dad, backing him away from me. This would end with one final, vile comment slung at me over his shoulder as he walked away, throwing his arms up as if we were all idiots.

My daughter labeled this, "chaos mode." This is a perfect description of what we witnessed, time and time again. Our abuser would yell and scream while we tried to figure out exactly what he wanted, always in vain as the demands were irrational and his thought pattern illogical. The answer seemed to change or be vague, making it impossible for us to figure out how to do what he wanted and therefore to calm him down. He was in chaos mode, and we were in survival mode.

Narcissists feel that rules don't apply to them. If they get caught breaking rules, they explain their actions with illogical thought patterns. This, of course, makes no sense to the person they offended.

I read about this but was still shocked at how brazen his behavior was as he ignored rules set forth by the judge in our divorce battle. One example was that we were told not to make any large purchases. As soon as I moved out with my Toyota Jetta, he bought a new car. He already had possession of two fairly new vehicles, but stated that he needed a small car for work.

People with NPD use "splitting" as a defense mechanism. Splitting is the unconscious act of seeing people as either all good or all bad. If the person with NPD sees you as all bad, he or she feels justified in abusing you, even in front of your children.

People with NPD are filled with shame. Shame from their underlying insecurity and inadequate sense of self. They self-soothe with immature and inadequate coping behaviors, such as over working, gambling, watching pornography, overeating, drinking alcohol, taking drugs, and overspending.

Interestingly, my abuser frequently said to me, "Shame on you!" when my opinion differed from his. This is a beautiful example of projection!

Narcissists have the mistaken assumption that they own their spouse and children. This was a common theme in our marriage, during the divorce, and even after the divorce. People with this personality disorder genuinely feel you are a part of them or an extension of them. This explains why they get so angry with you, seemingly for no reason. Since they believe your brain is controlled by theirs, they get angry when you don't move the right way or say the right thing. Of course, you have absolutely no idea what you have done wrong, so the anger seems to come out of nowhere.

This concept has been very difficult for me to accept. The unmitigated gall in assuming that my brain was his is beyond infuriating! My brain is mine!

"Why are you yelling?" I would ask occasionally. We would be having a seemingly innocuous conversation, and he would start yelling at me for something that seemed to be an entirely different topic. It was as if I had missed part of the conversation.

I would say, "I am not in your brain, so I have no idea how the conversation took that turn."

As I got sick of this scenario over the years, I changed that comment to, "I am not in your brain, thank God, so I have no idea what you are yelling about."

During the more than two decades that I observed Glen's narcissistic nuances, I became an accidental and unwilling expert in his game.

One of my abuser's nuanced mannerisms included making side comments about a topic mid-sentence. These comments would be his true feelings, often about a person, and they would be insolent, personal jabs. During the last few years, I have noted this same mannerism in other narcissists whom I have encountered in person or have listened to on different media outlets. I now call these "jackass comments" because they are usually mean and insensitive.

You know how you may have not-so-nice thoughts about the topic at hand, but your brain has a filter, so those thoughts don't come out of your mouth? Well, narcissists, with their underdeveloped emotional intelligence and lack of empathy, don't have that filter. Actually, it is probably not that they lack a filter but that they are intending to hurt you or someone else. And hurt they do.

If the narcissist feels a threat to the belief that they are perfect and deserve respect, they experience "narcissistic injury." This can lead to narcissistic rage, which is often disproportionate to the perceived threat.

On the following pages, you will find many examples of narcissistic injury resulting in narcissistic rage.

Chapter 14

Gaslighting: What is it?

Gaslighting is a form of manipulation in which the abuser presents a false narrative, which leads the victim to question the validity of their own thoughts, perception of reality, and memories. So, basically, it's when someone changes the story but doesn't tell you, and then acts like you are crazy when you don't remember it the same way.

Gaslighting is a common tactic used by people with NPD as they try to gain control of their victim.

The term gaslighting is a colloquialism that comes from the 1944 film called *Gaslight*. In this movie, Gregory (Charles Boyer) manipulates Paula (Ingrid Bergman).

Paula had been raised by her beloved aunt, as her mother had died shortly after she was born.

As a young child, Paula discovered her murdered aunt in their home, after she went down the stairs to investigate an unusual noise.

Much later, Paula met Gregory and he immediately started love-bombing her. She fell in love and married him.

He then convinced her to move back into her abandoned aunt's house, which she had inherited. Her aunt had been wealthy, and a rumor was circulating that jewels were hidden in the house.

Paula was reluctant, given her childhood trauma, but Gregory was persuasive.

Meanwhile, immediately after the wedding, Gregory started to isolate Paula. She did not even go outside for the first three months of their marriage.

He started to lay the groundwork that she was mentally ill, by telling the housemaid and cook that Paula was nervous and not well.

He told Paula that she was prone to losing things, after he had hidden a broach that he had just given her.

He told her that she imagined things, like his flirtation with the housemaid, which he blatantly did in her presence.

He then added that it pained him when she was not well and lost in her imagination. He asked her if she was becoming forgetful and paranoid. He also gaslighted her by saying that she believed he was treating her harshly—isolating her from others and keeping her confined. This was the truth, but he implied that she was acting delusional by thinking these things.

Gregory's goal was to get Paula admitted to a psychiatric facility so she would be out of his way, and he could more freely search for the hidden jewels.

The name "gaslight" comes from the plot line in which Gregory turned on the gaslight in the attic as he searched for the jewels. This caused the lights in the rest of the house to dim. When she would tell him this was happening, he led her to believe she was the only one who saw this happening.

This was Gregory changing the narrative so Paula would question her reality.

She became more and more depressed as the movie progressed. It is very sad to watch as a beautiful, vibrant, talented young woman is reduced to an isolated life in which she does not trust her own memory or perception of reality.

As this happened, Paula developed a "trauma bond" with Gregory, as he repetitively abused her and then offered comfort. By then, he had her so isolated from family, friends, and society that she had nobody else to turn to.

Paula was slowly and systematically driven out of her mind. She was not crazy though; Gregory's behavior was crazy-making.

This story is shockingly like my own, except there were no hidden jewels but rather a hard-working medical doctor who was making a good income.

Glen used gaslighting to manipulate me and our children for years. In the last few years of our marriage, it basically became the only form of communication between the two of us. I have frequently said that I used to "speak Glen," which I meant that I learned to follow the loose thread of truth that ran through his confabulated stories and blatant lies. I could somewhat follow the plot.

Through all this, I was somehow able to continue to trust my own memory. My mind adapted to automatically memorize full conversations. When Glen would contradict what happened, I would repeat the conversation to him. This was to no avail, as he would continue to say my version was wrong. I often wished our conversations were videotaped, so he could see how it really went. As I studied this disorder, I learned that people with NPD do not like to be taped. This makes sense. Why would they want anything available that could potentially prove them wrong? They can't be wrong. It just doesn't work that way.

Chapter 15

A Marriage Full of Gaslighting

The gaslighting was insidious initially, but it didn't stay that way because I was living with a narcissist. His manipulation with gaslighting became so pervasive, that I eventually felt like it had taken over every aspect of my home life.

I attempted to untangle this mess in my mind by writing my story and I hope this helps you on your journey. Are you enmeshed with a narcissist? Maybe one or several of these examples will feel familiar.

You will note some disorganization or chaos with some of the stories because that is actually how they played out.

You will also note horrible grammar and sentence structure in some of the quotes from Glen, as they are actual quotes from what he said or texted.

I will tell this story in chronological order, starting when our children were young. I will occasionally backtrack further to provide context.

⚜

We have four children. Molly is the oldest and the only daughter. Next are Charles, Sawyer, and then Hunter.

When Molly was six, Charles four, and Sawyer two, Glen decided we needed a dog. I was busy with my medical practice and raising the three children. I told Glen we didn't have time for a dog, as it takes a lot of work to train them appropriately. Whenever I didn't agree with what Glen wanted, he would proceed with his plan and later tell me, "We talked about it."

To which I would respond, "Yes, we talked about it, and I did not agree."

He searched the internet and found a private person selling the breed of hunting dog he wanted. He scheduled an appointment, and we all traveled to the location. When we arrived, it appeared the dogs were older than advertised. They were very ill mannered, barking and jumping up on the fence and then on us.

Glen announced, "We are going to buy two of them."

I said, "Umm, what? That is a bad idea as they are clearly out of control dogs, and they are not puppies."

Glen said the seller privately told him the dogs would be euthanized if we didn't buy them. Of course, I was with them both the whole time we were at the seller's place, so I knew this was a lie.

I said, "Why doesn't he give them to us for free then, just to have them off his hands so he doesn't have to euthanize them?"

"That is not how this works."

Oh, okay, I thought sarcastically, *there is a protocol for this exact scenario apparently and I am just the moron who doesn't understand that.*

Discussion over.

Glen conveniently forgot his checkbook, so he had me write the check for the dogs.

When the dogs turned out to be untrainable, Glen told me, "You bought them, so this is your fault."

"What? I said not to buy them. They were too old."

"You wrote the check."

One day, the dogs disappeared. He told me and the kids, "They both ran away. I called for them when they ran across the field, but they kept running."

⚜

On the day that our youngest child, Hunter, was born, a huge thunderstorm damaged several mature trees on our property.

When Glen left the hospital that night, I told him to call someone about the tree removal, as I knew that was an inherently dangerous job.

The next morning, Glen had the neighbor girl come babysit so he could remove the trees himself. As he was using the chainsaw, a large tree branch fell on him, entrapping him and injuring his arm and knee.

He was able to free himself and crawl to the door. The babysitter called an ambulance, and he was brought to the emergency department (ED) of the hospital where I had just given birth. I was on my way to meet him in the ED when the nurse came to inform me that our infant had briefly stopped breathing in the nursery. I knew Glen was in good hands in the ED and would be getting tests done, so I changed course and met the pediatrician in the nursery. Fortunately, Hunter was fine and just needed to be monitored for an additional day.

By the time the pediatrician finished his exam, ran some tests, and explained the situation to me, Glen had been moved from the ED to a hospital room. A nurse was able to take me by wheelchair to a different part of our large hospital so I could see him. We all eventually got home. I was healing, taking care of a newborn and three other children, and tending to Glen, who was camped out on the living room recliner with his injured arm and leg. About three nights into this debacle, I was up about 2 a.m. feeding the baby and changing his diaper. I heard Glen calling my name, so I went down to the living room to see what he needed. He wanted ice for his arm, which I got. He then started yelling at me because I wasn't doing enough for him. At the end of his diatribe, he ordered, "Just go."

I stood there for several seconds, unable to move or speak. I had a tingling sensation from my head to my toes. I felt acutely overwhelmed with my life. Not just the new baby and the fact that I was in a healing postpartum state myself while the asshole in my life was demanding my care, but my entire life.

I was in a functional freeze state, which is a psychological response to my overwhelming stress. After several seconds, I regained my ability to move. I turned around, went back up the stairs, got back into bed, and curled up into a ball. I started crying uncontrollably. I had nothing more to give and I was trapped. I was trapped because I could not save myself without leaving my children alone with this absolute monster. Trapped!

I worked more than a typical full-time schedule but was dedicated to exclusively breastfeeding my children. This was important to me, and I felt blessed to be able to do it. When I gave birth to Hunter, the hospital gifted us a goodie-bag that included a sample of baby formula. Certainly, it was from a company attempting to get new mothers to choose their brand. I had this in our cupboard for emergencies but had a stock of my breastmilk in the freezer. Despite the full stock and the fact that Glen knew I worked hard to keep Hunter exclusively breastfed, he decided to feed him the formula one day while I was at work.

Hunter gagged when he tasted the formula. Gagging caused a drop in his heart rate and blood pressure, a vasovagal response. This caused him to briefly lose consciousness.

"Dad freaked out, got us in the car, and handed Hunter to me to hold while he drove," recalled Molly, who was eight years old.

Please note that Glen had Molly hold Hunter in her lap, rather than putting him in a car seat, as he sped to the emergency department! The pure idiocy of this astounds me!

He told Molly, "Keep him awake or he'll die!"

Fortunately, they all made it to the ED alive, but Molly remains traumatized by this event to this day.

Glen carried Hunter into the emergency department and, according to my traumatized daughter, left once the nurse was getting Hunter settled into a room. He just left! He didn't tell them he was leaving; he just left a five-month-old infant in the emergency department and drove across the street to my office!

He sauntered into my medical clinic with the other three kids in tow. The clinic was closed as it was after 5 p.m., so a fellow neurologist, Jenny, and I were the only ones there.

The back door was near Jenny's office, so Glen stopped and had a conversation with her, as if nothing was wrong and he was in no hurry. He then worked his way to my office, while still calmly chatting with her as she walked beside him and the kids.

When I saw Glen, I greeted him and the kids.

Confused, I looked around and said, "Where is Hunter?"

Glen said, "He is in the emergency room." That was the end of his explanation.

I waited a couple seconds and when I realized he was not going to provide further information, I impatiently asked, "What? Why is he in the emergency room?"

"He passed out," he said in a monotone voice, as if this were not something to be concerned about.

I looked at Jenny in horror, grabbed the three kids, and quickly headed out the door. We ran across the street and rushed into the emergency department, while Glen went to move the car. The emergency physician, whom I knew, looked at me with relief and gently placed my baby in my arms. She told me everything was looking fine but they wanted to monitor him for a couple hours.

She added, "We didn't know where Hunter's dad went."

I tried to maintain composure in front of my colleague, but I had so many conflicting emotions. I was relieved that Hunter was fine, but I was colliding head-on into the realization that Glen was incapable of safely caring for our kids. He had no job and zero desire to get one. He was actually actively trying not to get a job, despite my pleading.

I was financially supporting the family of six and we certainly couldn't survive without my income if I were to stay home to care for the kids. It was then that I realized I was trapped, overwhelmed, and scared as hell.

Jenny still talks about how strange and scary this incident was, on so many levels. Glen had no insight into the fact that the baby should have been in a car seat. He had no insight into the fact that you can't leave an infant in the emergency department without a parent. He had no insight into the fact that he should have told the nurse where he was going. He had no insight into the fact that he should have immediately given me the information about where Hunter was and what was transpiring. He had no insight into the fact that he should have just called me to meet him in the ED. He had no insight into the fact that you don't tell an eight-year-old that her brother would die if she didn't keep him awake.

While coming to the realization that my relationship with Glen was not sustainable, I was simultaneously aware that I could not leave my young children alone with this moron for days at a time if we got divorced. Trapped!

⚜

During the time that Glen was a "stay-at-home dad," he took a three-week Alaskan moose hunting trip.

I put his title in quotations as Glen was simply nothing more than a man without a job. Calling him a stay-at-home dad does a huge injustice to this title.

During the extensive time that he was a man without a job, he spent months planning a moose hunting trip and presented it to me as a one-week trip. A few days before he left, he casually informed me it was a three-week trip. The kids were young, ranging from infant to nine years old, and I was working full time. I had only scheduled one week off from work so I could take care of the kids while he was gone. This was also right when school was starting, so this left me with school orientations to attend for the three older children, in addition to my multiple other responsibilities as a mother, business owner, physician, and homeowner.

Glen arranged for his actively alcoholic father to take care of Hunter during the day for the two weeks that I would be back at work. So, I went to work the day after I found out his actual hunting plan and blocked any open appointment spots and rearranged my schedule as best I could so I could be home as much as possible. I contorted around the schedule of a "stay-at-home dad."

※

Let's fast-forward in our story to when Molly was thirteen, Charles was eleven, Sawyer was nine, and Hunter was five years old. We went on a ski trip with Maria and Jacob, who were now married, and we occasionally traveled with them and their two children.

I was skiing with Maria and Jacob, while Glen was skiing

with Hunter. The other kids were skiing in a pack, likely taking jumps the parents did not want to witness.

Glen was skiing ahead of Hunter, which I never did, as there was no way to keep an eye on him from that vantage point. He was only five! Hunter turned down a side path as Glen skied, in total oblivion, further down the mountain.

When Hunter realized he lost Glen, he found someone from ski patrol and told them, "I lost my dad."

Hunter had memorized our cell phone numbers and he recited Glen's number to ski patrol. They called Glen immediately, so he was aware that Hunter had been found. Glen told them to just bring Hunter to me at the chalet, as he knew it was time for our appointed meeting time for lunch with everyone.

By this point, Maria, Jacob, and I were waiting in the chalet, visiting at a large table. I looked over Jacob's shoulder and was shocked to see Hunter walk in with two men from ski patrol. Hunter saw me, ran to me, and started crying as his emotions released. One of the men told me what happened, gave Hunter a high five, and praised his skiing skills.

I praised my little boy for being aware enough to look for ski patrol right when he realized he was lost. I asked him how he knew who worked for ski patrol, and he explained that they wear red coats with a white cross on them. I have often thought about how things could have gone very differently if Hunter had not made this observation earlier in the day.

I then called Glen and asked if he and Hunter were almost to the chalet for lunch.

He responded, "I am almost there, but Hunter is in a ski lesson."

I coldly remarked, "He is here with me. Ski patrol dropped him off and told me he had been lost."

Glen said, "Okay, I will be there in a minute." Then he hung up.

No expression of relief that he was with me. No change in story or admission of the lie. Just done. End of discussion. End of story.

Maria and Jacob, having witnessed this whole gaslighting incident, sat in stunned disbelief.

Maria said, "That was not okay! I would have been so mad!"

I, however, knew that any further discussion was futile and would only lead to more gaslighting, so I had to just swallow my anger. Swallow my anger and continue to count down the days, years, until I could leave the bastard.

I hated riding in a car with Glen, as he would tailgate and drive at excessive speeds. He did this from the time I met him, and it always made me nervous. Aggressive driving is common amongst narcissists. This comes from their sense of entitlement, the feeling that rules don't apply to them, and from their lack of empathy for others.

We were in the car with all the kids, on a two-lane curvy highway at night. Glen was driving eighty-five miles per hour. I looked at the speedometer and told him to slow down.

He told me, "I am not even driving very fast."

"You are going eighty-five miles per hour in a fifty-five mile per hour zone."

Molly was in the back seat and said, "The iPad is saying you are going eighty-five miles per hour."

"Stop and let us out!" I told him. I didn't have a plan for the five of us on a road that I was not familiar with, but I did not want to stay in that car.

He did not stop, but did slow down to about seventy miles per hour.

⚘

This particular year, I was on call for the weekend. As I previously described, on call days were very busy. When on call for the weekend, I was on from 8 a.m. Saturday to 8 a.m. Monday.

Weekend call responsibilities consisted of rounding on everyone's current hospitalized patients, taking patient and physician phone calls, seeing new hospital consults, and covering neurologic issues in the emergency room. Call was very busy, very stressful, and very unpredictable.

So, I was scheduled to be on call the weekend of the pheasant hunting season opener. Glen wanted to host his entire family for supper Saturday evening. His family is very large, at that time consisting of about forty people. We were already having five of his family and friends from Kansas City staying at our house for the weekend. We discussed this a few weeks prior to the event and I told him that the plan for us hosting supper was not possible. This shouldn't have been an issue, as several of his siblings live in the same area and could have easily hosted it.

The weekend arrived and the men from Kansas City settled in. Early the next morning, they all milled around our property getting everything ready for the 10 a.m. start time, while I left for work.

I returned home from the hospital later that evening, after being at work for about ten hours.

Glen called shortly after I got home and said, "Check the chili in the man-shed."

"Are you having people over—"

Click. He hung up.

I called him back immediately, multiple times, but he didn't answer.

I went to the shed and found a huge crock pot filled with chili. The plan was obviously for the full party to occur at our house.

I felt so aggravated that my whole body was vibrating. I had unreleased energy that had no pressure release because Glen would not answer the phone. My fight or flight response was in high gear.

I felt frustrated and helpless at my "partner's" inability to communicate.

I felt outrage at the blatant disregard for me when he planned this party.

I felt ill that he wasn't man enough to even tell me the party was happening.

I also felt like I had to quickly get my shit together and get my emotions in check, as people would be arriving soon.

Glen and a few other men arrived home about one hour later. I found Glen in the garage unloading our dog.

I said, as calmly as I could, "I need to talk to you."

He didn't look at me, but said, "I have too much to do."

He walked away, with a running water hose in his hand, to spray off the dead pheasants in the driveway.

I stepped on the hose, causing it to yank out of his hand. He stopped and glared at me.

"Are you having a party here?" I asked through gritted teeth.

He answered, "Yes, this is my house, and I can have a party"

He turned from me and walked away. Discussion over.

His family, plus several friends arrived, and the party of forty to fifty adults and children went into full swing.

Shortly after they arrived, I was called to the hospital and left. I was happy to have a good excuse to leave, as I was not able to pretend everything was okay for even another minute.

The next year, opening pheasant weekend was a "same song, second verse" situation.

The week before the event, I texted Glen, "What is the plan for this weekend?'

He answered, "I am having a party at our house."

"I didn't know anything about this, and I am again on call."

Glen replied, "It is already all planned. It has been planned for a year, including the menu."

I became rightfully angry, as I had again been excluded from this decision. I only found out when I did because I had asked about it.

He finished our text exchange with, "It is your fault because you don't communicate with me."

Everything was always somehow my fault.

When his family started to arrive, I was heading out the door to return to the hospital.

My sister-in-law asked where I was going and was surprised that I was going to work when the party was about to start. I told her I had just learned of the party plan, so I was not able to change my call schedule. She looked surprised and said, "But there were several emails about this."

I sighed, and flatly stated, "Yep, I just learned about that today too. This is how my life goes with Glen."

She shrugged and said, "Well, that's Glen."

"Yep," echoed Glen's mother, who was standing beside her and also shrugged.

I had heard this response for years from his family members. In short, this response told me they knew he was like this; he was never going to change, and I would just need to deal with it. But my ability to accept this behavior and pretend was waning . . . quickly.

The same night of this party, I had just gotten home and was in our room finishing a note on a patient.

Hunter rushed into my room. He was pale, hyperventilating and whimpering. He had a large cut on the inside of his leg from climbing and then sliding down a post. The post had a large, dirty hook that was used to hang dead animals. Yes, I was living in hell with a total hick!

I needed to quickly get Hunter to the emergency department. I went out to the garage, got my son in the car, then opened the garage door to discover several cars in my way. I had to yell over the noise of the drunken bonfire to get people to move their cars.

I drove Hunter to the emergency department (ED). Shortly after we left, our sister-in-law volunteered to bring Glen to meet us at the hospital. He had had too much to drink, so it was not an option for him to drive.

Hunter and I were in the triage area at the hospital, which had a good view of the entrance. Car lights flashed as a vehicle drove into the parking lot, just as Glen called, asking where we were.

I told him, "We are in the ED. Just come in the ED door."

He said, "I am in the ED, where are you?"

"You are not in the ED. I can see the entry door and waiting room."

"I am in the emergency room. Did you go to the other hospital?"

"Come in the door and you will see us with the nurse." I remained on the phone with him as I watched him walk in the door. I said, "Look straight ahead."

Surprise of all surprises, we were right there!

This is an overt example of the trouble an NPD has with the truth. And this was classic gaslighting as he attempted to alter my reality.

While Hunter was getting Novocain and then stitches, I kept my face close to his. I was calmly talking to him and stroking his hair.

I stopped talking briefly and Hunter said, "Keep talking to me." It was clearly calming him.

Glen looked at me and said, "Let's have some quiet time."

Hunter looked at me with pleading, scared eyes and said, "Keep talking to me, Mom." Glen was texting his friends and family during this time instead of offering comfort and support to our child. He was obviously intoxicated, and this was embarrassing in my place of employment.

When Charles was a sophomore in high school, he accidently bumped our Suburban with his Jetta while backing up in our driveway. The Jetta was manual with a stick shift and Charles thought the slight bump he felt while backing up was from popping into first gear from reverse.

Glen had a full-blown gaslighting incident with this accident and made up an elaborate story.

He called me at work and stated, "Charles was in a parking lot in town and his music was loud. He backed into a car and drove away. The guy he hit is going to press charges for a hit and run unless Charles apologizes."

"Who did he hit?" I asked. "Is it someone we know? How much damage was there?"

"I am not telling you."

"Why?" I asked.

"I gotta go." *Click.*

You may be noticing the common occurrence of Glen hanging up on me when he was done with what he wanted to say. I was frequently mid-sentence when I would realize that nobody was on the other end of the line.

Since I would acquire no additional information, I had to finish my workday with this vague but serious incident hanging over my head, wondering if my son was going to be arrested.

When I got home from work, Glen was not there. I discussed the situation with Molly and Charles. Even Charles, who Glen said was involved in the accident, could not figure out what Glen was talking about.

We looked at the back of the vehicle Charles had been driving and saw no damage, not even a scratch.

Molly was only seventeen years old, but she already had insight into Glen's thought process. She said, "There is a thread of truth to everything Dad says. We just have to find the thread and figure it out."

The three of us began hypothesizing at the source of this accusation. As we worked on this, Glen sent us a picture. He said it was from the person whose vehicle was hit. The picture showed a small back section of a vehicle, with a finger pointing to the damage.

Molly realized the picture was the Suburban and the shadow of the person taking the picture was her father. The "damage" was a miniscule indentation that was barely visible. I wasn't even certain it was new. This vehicle was a few years old by this time.

Glen arrived home but did not want to discuss this with us. After several hours and with increasing pressure from Molly for the truth, Glen admitted this was our Suburban and that it had happened in our driveway.

He fell back on his typical response when he was actually caught in a lie. He said, "It was a joke."

I replied, "How is that possibly funny on any level? I thought my child was in trouble with the law."

He then changed his rationale to, "I was teaching Charles a lesson."

I quickly retorted, "Maybe the next time you decide to teach our children a lesson, you could let me in on the plan rather than leading me to believe our child was going to be arrested."

Molly worked through this gaslighting incident with persistence and precision. She was learning how to live with a narcissist! As I recall this incident, I remember feeling both proud and saddened that she was beginning to "speak Glen."

✼

On my fiftieth birthday, I was on my way to Minneapolis to help Molly look for an apartment for her upcoming college year.

Glen called me fourteen times in forty-five minutes because he was arguing with the oldest two boys. I know it was that many times because my nephew was riding in the car with me and started to count after about the sixth call. He had not grown up with this type of behavior and found it obnoxious.

I tried to understand the story Glen was describing so I could attempt to help from 100 miles away. Alas, it was fruitless as he was speaking irrationally and yelling at the kids while I was on the phone with him.

Glen sent me a close-up picture of two vehicles, his and Charles's.

He called me right after I received the picture and said, "The boys blocked my car, so I can't drive out of the parking lot. It is very dangerous! Tell them to just listen to me!"

I called Charles, who stated simply, "It is actually Dad's vehicle that is blocking us in."

Glen was projecting his poor behavior as he blamed others. Nothing was ever his fault, and he was always the victim.

✼

Glen was always a horrid gift giver.

I came home from work to an empty house and found my bike in the kitchen. This was a bike that I had not used for several years. I had bought it before we were even married; it was used and old.

On this day, Glen had gotten it down from our garage attic and cleaned it up a little, very little.

Maria called while I was pondering the bike in my kitchen. By this time, I was well aware of Glen's gift-giving skills, so I said, "I think this might be my birthday present."

She laughed and said, "Well, it better have some bling attached to it then."

So, as predicted, the bike was for my birthday. He didn't put a bow on it or even tell me about it until I asked why the bike was in the house. He then said, "It is your birthday present."

When I looked confused at how a bike I bought could be a present from him, he added, "I had it restored."

I found this odd, as there was a rip in the seat and rust on the metal showing beneath the padding.

A few months later, I took it to a bike shop to get it ready for an upcoming triathlon. The chain was squeaking, and the tires were literally disintegrating.

As the owner of the shop was bending down inspecting the bike, I informed him that my husband had it restored a few months ago.

The owner looked at me and smirked, "Nobody has worked on this bike for years."

I was immediately embarrassed, but that was quickly followed by sadness. I was embarrassed that Glen's fake story made me publicly look like an idiot. I was sad because, well, it was just so sad. The sadness was deep within my heart as I fought off tears in the bike shop. My husband was supposed to love me, yet he lied to me and didn't feel I was worthy of a birthday gift.

My self-worth and self-esteem took another hit in that moment, another chink in my armor and another win for an NPD as I dove further into despair.

For years, Glen continued to tell me this was a thoughtful present. In his sick mind, I guess he had rationalized that it was. I made a rule after that gift: "No shopping on our property." You wouldn't think this would need to be stated, but it is a valid comment when dealing with NPD.

One summer, Glen drove our tractor about five miles down the road to help an acquaintance, not really a friend but an acquaintance, plant his large lawn.

During this time that he was trying to impress others with his kindness instead of tilling my garden, the tractor broke down. He called me to come get him.

When I was driving him home, I asked, "Are you charging them for this work?"

He didn't look at me but answered, "Yes."

"How much?"

"None of your business," he said matter-of-factly.

A few minutes later, he was lamenting on how much it would cost to fix the tractor, and he said, "This is why you don't do things for free."

Oops! He had forgotten to keep track of his lies, as gaslighting is very convoluted and confusing.

One fall, we were preparing for our annual cross-country team party at our house. Charles was eighteen and Sawyer was sixteen and they were both on the team, so this was a party to celebrate them and their teammates. I had everything prepared the previous day, as I was scheduled to work right up to the start of the party.

Glen had not helped with the preparations at all, but he knew the kids and I would be busy with last-minute details.

About two hours before the party, he insisted that Sawyer do a lawn-mowing job that afternoon, rather than the next day when Sawyer had planned to do it.

On a normal day, this lawn-mowing job was always a logistical fiasco because Glen had a rule that only he was able to drive with the trailer to take the lawnmower to the site.

So, on this day, in his usual fashion, Glen was asking the impossible. He wanted Sawyer to do the lawn right away; to a person with NPD, everything is an emergency.

As a result, Sawyer called me several times because Glen was yelling and causing chaos while working on last-minute party details at the house. Then, about an hour before the party was to start, Glen drove Sawyer to the site.

Meanwhile, I finished seeing my patients and left my charting for later, as I rushed to help my child. I drove to the lawn mowing site, where I witnessed Glen being irrational and yelling at Sawyer. He was telling Sawyer that he was doing the job incorrectly, even though this was a job that Sawyer had been doing for two years.

By this point, Sawyer was incredibly frustrated, and he was trying not to break down in tears.

Sawyer did the job and was about forty-five minutes late for his own cross-country party.

It was heart-wrenching to witness this. I was helpless in getting Glen to stop verbally abusing my child. The very person that was supposed to love and protect him, was hurting him.

I was starting to hate Glen for this continued abuse of me and my children. Actual hate, not just slight dislike. I hated him to my core!

Chapter 16

Just Mean

About fifteen years into our marriage, we were snow skiing with Maria and Jacob. I was having trouble getting my goggles to stay down on the back of my helmet because the strap that held it down had come loose. I was not able to get one end of the plastic strap into the little hole.

I asked Glen to try to fix it and turned around so he could see the back of my head, where the strap was loose. The helmet was on my head and Glen tried to push the plastic piece into the little hole. He then, without warning, hit the helmet three times in rapid succession with the base of his open hand. This was so hard that I heard my neck make a crunching sound.

I turned and said, "What are you doing? That hurt!"

He turned and skied away.

My initial reaction was embarrassment, because this had occurred in front of Maria and the chalet filled with skiers. I then felt incredibly sad. I skied away, with Maria following, as the tears flowed down my face. Maria gave me a hug when we stopped, and said, "That was not okay."

Glen was just plain mean and uncaring. He didn't give a shit about anyone. His only concern was for what he wanted at the time. He was unable, or unwilling, to read a room or situation. One weekend, just as the sun was coming up, I was asleep in our bedroom. I could vaguely hear Glen opening the window on my side of the bed. This was slightly annoying because it was a rare day that I could sleep in.

Suddenly, and without warning, there was a deafening gunshot, two feet from my head! I bolted upright with wild eyes, my heart racing, my limbic system fully activated. I focused; Glen was pointing a gun out the window.

My fear turned quickly to anger. Fear and anger are located adjacent to each other in the brain, so one can activate the other very quickly. He glanced at me with an expression of annoyance, as if my confusion, fear, and anger were ridiculous. As if this were normal behavior and I was simply being irrational and uptight.

I exclaimed, "What the fuck are you doing?"

He looked at me and scolded, "You need to calm down and get rid of the potty mouth. There was a racoon in the yard."

We lived in the country, on thirty-two acres of land, in South Dakota. Of course, there was wildlife in the yard.

He left the room, leaving me to sort out what had just happened inside my house. I tried to slow my heart rate, not just from the gunshot, but from the fact that I was living a nightmare. This was not just odd and eccentric behavior; this was a deranged man! And he had several guns in the house.

This. Happened. Twice!

Chapter 17

He Refused to Get a Job

We started marriage counseling eventually, and by this, I mean after about eighteen years of marriage. At that time, I naively thought the primary issue in our marriage was Glen's refusal to get a job. Our issues were so much deeper.

People with NPD tend to fall into two categories when it comes to work: too much or not at all. I was married to a not-at-all NPD!

Glen did different jobs in the early years of our marriage, but quit his job when our long-time nanny got married and moved. At the time, we had three children, ages five, three, and one.

The decision for him to be a stay-at-home dad was initially sort of a mutual decision. It sounded logical for me to be the one working, as I could make more money than he could. However, as we explored Glen becoming the primary caretaker, my intuition was screaming, *This is a bad idea!* I tried to figure out what was unsettling for me and decided it was simply that I wanted to spend more time with the kids myself.

Was I just feeling jealous? It is common for the partner of an NPD to feel like they are the one at fault, and that is definitely what I felt frequently. So, yes, at that moment I acknowledged to myself that I was feeling jealous.

As I look back, I see that was not the case and my brain was sending out warning signals that I just couldn't interpret at that point in my life. Eventually, the answer to my distress became apparent. He never wanted to return to work. He wanted me to do all the work *ad infinitum*.

I started working even more as the only wage earner, typically fifty to seventy hours per week. My time with the kids was limited because of my work hours, which I loathed. So, I would spend all evening with them and then stay up late, working into the night to get everything done from the day and preparing for the next day. It felt like an endless marathon. More than a marathon really, since even an ultra-marathon eventually ends.

In direct contrast, Glen would typically fall asleep on the couch shortly after I got home in the evening and then move up to bed about 1 a.m.

Glen did not hold a steady job for eleven years. He did odd jobs, but those amounted to next to nothing.

By this time, our kids were sixteen, fourteen, twelve, and eight. So, they were well past the age of needing a stay-at-home dad. Now,

I am aware this set-up works well for many families, but it was not working for our family, and I had made this known to Glen.

When I told him that I had enough and that he needed to contribute to the family finances, he told me he was looking for a job, but he would not, or could not, provide specifics.

"Have you set up any interviews?" I would ask.

His response was, "You don't even know how to get a job."

There were certain comments he made that left me literally speechless, and this was one of them. Not only did I have a job, but I was also co-owner of a business in which I regularly hired employees.

Idiot!

He eventually got a job when Hunter was in third grade.

He was never proud of being a stay-at-home dad. When asked about his job, he would state his prior job. His LinkedIn profile still hides the eleven years out of work. He technically worked unscheduled part time and had a small weed-spraying business during those years, but this amounted to a few days of work per year. Let me emphasize, this was per *year*, not per week or per month!

After he finally got a job, I was constantly worried that it wouldn't last. Of course, my concerns were warranted and then validated.

One evening Molly, Glen, and I were outside on the patio.

Glen stood up as if leaving and said, "I am going to quit my job and work part time. I don't have time to go to all the kids' activities."

I said, "That is not ideal because we get insurance with your job. If we go back to insurance from my work, it is much more expensive, as I am self-employed."

"It is not your decision, it is mine." And he walked away. Discussion over.

At sixteen, Molly was old enough to realize, in her gut, that this is not a normal response from a partner and still recalls the discomfort of this interaction. I suspect, with her intuition, she was also picking up on my unspoken distress.

Once again, I would be the one to carry the majority of the financial burden for our family. It was always me by default.

On top of shirking responsibility on the financial front, Glen was also unwilling to do his part in the home. I did essentially all the cleaning, grocery shopping, cooking, laundry, clothes shopping, and homework assistance. I sorted through backpacks, made school lunches, and made sure everything was ready for the next school day. I set up and attended all medical doctor and dental visits.

He, meanwhile, did the yard work and his own laundry. He usually did his chores on the weekends while I cared for the kids, rather than doing it during the week when he was home alone.

He tried to get me to do his laundry, by throwing it in the huge pile I would make by the laundry machine on Saturday mornings. I would then work my way through about six loads as the day progressed. But I separated his clothes out and put them back in the laundry bin. It was my tiny rebellion. And what the hell, anyway? Seriously, what the actual hell?

Oddly, he would randomly do my laundry. I told him not to do this, as I air-dry several of my clothing items.

He continued to randomly do it, though, and to put all my stuff in the dryer. He would leave it in the dryer for me to find and I am sure he enjoyed the aggravation it caused every single time.

Right after I filed for divorce, he did this more often and then he stopped doing it. But why? Something was up, but what was it? Did he stop the laundry war, or just change tactics? He changed tactics.

When I was in the process of doing my laundry, he would yell at me the minute the washer or dryer stopped. He would tell me to move my laundry. This was his control. In his mind, the washer and dryer were his and I was just allowed to borrow them.

I would eventually learn that there was even more trouble with the stay-at-home dad title. The simple fact that Glen was unemployed made him the inappropriately titled primary caregiver. That was black and white in family law in our state at the time I was going through this.

But really, why use your brain and the truth to make a family law decision on something as important as who children will spend most of their time with?

It didn't matter that there was no valid reason he was not working; he just didn't want to. And it didn't matter that the reason I was working was because I had no other option if my family was to survive.

When I initially sought legal counsel to consider divorce, I learned I would likely only have custody of the children every other weekend.

I was trapped in this marriage! In the twenty-first century in the United States of America, I was trapped in a marriage!

There was no way I could leave my children, who were very young at that time. I needed to wait until they were at least able to be physically safe when they were with Glen for long periods of time.

It is also common for the partner of a narcissist to over-function in the family, particularly if the partner is someone who needs order, which is very true for me. To maintain order, I had to do everything, or it simply was not going to get done. This was very exhausting, and I often felt like I was on the verge of everything falling apart.

In addition, once the partner takes over a chore, the narcissist will not take it back. It was a snowball that became an avalanche.

Chapter 18

He Put Himself First

Glen watched out for himself first, second, and third.

One December, my entire extended family was at our house for our yearly Christmas weekend celebration. This consisted of eighteen guests in addition to our family of four. I was pregnant with Sawyer and had two-year-old Charles and four-year-old Molly. Two hours before the family meal, I was rushing to get everything prepared in the kitchen.

Glen got a call from a friend asking him if he wanted to play basketball. He accepted the invitation! So, he thought absolutely nothing of leaving the entire family that had already gathered. He felt zero responsibility to help me prepare the meal or even to take care of his two children while

I did so. Also, he had not played basketball for the entire time I had known him! I had never seen him shoot a basket.

He headed to our bedroom and started to change into his workout clothes. I walked in and literally pleaded with him to stay and help me.

He ignored my pleas and stated, "I am going." He finished getting ready and walked out the door.

I went to our bathroom and, despite my efforts to shove the intense feelings into an already overflowing box at the back of my brain for later, I started to cry.

My entire family was downstairs, and I was crying in the bathroom.

My older sister, Kay, came into the bathroom, saw the look of despair on my face, and hugged me as I told her what was transpiring.

I told her, "This marriage is never going to last. I can't do this."

This was the first time I had said this out loud and it was devastating to realize my life was out of my control. I was deeply entangled in this mess and couldn't see a way out. I felt like a caged animal, pacing back and forth, but with no ability to release my intense feelings. This feeling would recur in the years to come, but at this point in my life, it was still relatively new.

Kay held me until I was done crying, and then we went downstairs and finished the meal preparations together.

Glen returned about an hour and a half later, acting as if everything was fine. Acting as if he wasn't a total asshole.

At the time, the thought of leaving was more overwhelming than the reality of staying. This was more than a decade before I had the courage to leave.

As I have said, Glen was a terrible gift giver but would buy lavish gifts for himself. On the day of my fiftieth birthday, Glen bought himself a new Glock gun.

I learned about this purchase during the divorce process, as I was going through the checks from his bank account.

He already owned twenty-seven guns and he never discussed any of these purchases with me.

Incidentally, when the appraiser came during the divorce process, only seven guns were located on our property. Only seven to account for as we divided up our property.

Also, two months after I filed for divorce, Glen texted my brother, "Forty-five semi auto grizzly mag just saying do not tell Cb. just got the gun."

My brother, of course, sent me that text. Glen seriously thought, in true narcissist fashion, that my brother was on his side of this battle.

I recently came across a letter from 1996, one year after I completed my neurology residency. This letter was from the editor of a leading headache journal. This world-renowned headache expert had read my article, published in a state medical journal, about the treatment of migraines during pregnancy and breastfeeding. He complimented the article and asked that I continue to write and contribute to this important area of study. I recall getting that letter and being very honored and proud.

I primarily focus on headache management in the field of neurology, and I love to write, but I was busy surviving as a hold was placed on my needs. I never published any other articles as the lead author.

This letter forced me to ponder what I could have accomplished in my field had I chosen a good, or even adequate, partner, had I been able to ever put my needs ahead of his.

Chapter 19

Empathy

Empathy is the ability to understand and vicariously experience the feelings of another person. If you have empathy, you are aware of someone's feelings and you are sensitive to them. Think of how you feel when someone explains their own sad experience to you. That feeling is normal. Narcissists do not have the ability to feel that.

As previously explained, perpetual dread has lived in me since Shon died when I was twenty-two years old. This became a convenient landmine for my abuser to inflict incredible pain upon my traumatized heart.

Here's an example. One day, when Charles was sixteen, he was late for curfew. He wasn't answering his phone, and I was hopeful that this was because he had been instructed to not be on his phone while driving. I started my anxious pacing from window to window, looking for his car or the dreaded red flashing lights.

I told Glen I was anxious because Charles was late. Instead of attempting to decrease my anxiety, he chose this as an opportunity to hurt me.

He said, "For all we know, he could be dead in a ditch somewhere."

Thwack! My skilled predator's arrow penetrated my sternum and went straight for my broken heart. Perfect shot!

That was the absolute worst thing to say to me, and he knew it. He knew my life had forever changed in a ditch.

This man was incapable of empathy. He could not feel any of my pain. I find this interesting about narcissists because they do intellectually know when something is painful for someone, as they are able to identify this and then use it to inflict pain on their victims.

Without empathy, you are really unable to share love with others. Eventually I realized that Glen didn't love me and could only love himself. There were several emotionally painful incidents in which he proved this to me. I will share a particularly glaring example from when Hunter was about eight, Sawyer was twelve, Charles was fourteen and Molly was sixteen.

We were at a cross-country meet, watching Molly, Charles, and Sawyer compete. The kids attended a fairly small school, so even though Sawyer was in seventh grade, he was fast and competed at the high school level.

Cross-country meets were usually at golf courses in our area, but this one was at a horse polo field and in the surrounding hills. Watching a cross-country meet is different from most sports, as there are no bleachers. If you want to see the competitors once or twice, you can stand at the start line and then walk to the finish line.

My way of watching was much more active and involved athletic wear, a backpack, and running shoes. I would watch the start and then sprint to the back of the course, to cheer on the kids where the crowd was sparse. I would then sprint back to the finish line. I am not fast, but I would cut corners to shorten my running distance.

With this particular event, I was cutting through a field with long grass, running beside Glen. There was a post hole that had been dug but no post had been placed in it. The hole was not visible in the tall grass. I stepped down and my right leg suddenly had no earth beneath it. I fell into the hole up to my thigh. This caused me to stop short, and my body fell forward. I was deep enough that I couldn't get out without effort.

I called out to Glen to help me out of the hole. He turned and saw me on the ground, laughed, turned back toward the direction he had been heading, and kept running. A friend who saw this happen walked over and gave me his hand to help me out of the hole.

I felt embarrassed, both that I had fallen and that I was not even worthy of assistance or love from my husband. I could barely keep from crying as I walked with my friend to continue cheering for the kids.

This was a low point for me. I was crushed. Any hope I held for the state of my husband's feelings toward me were dashed. A good husband, hell even an adequate one, would have made sure I was okay. A good husband would have helped me out of the hole. A good husband would have realized I was four months into marathon training, and I would be worried about an injury to my leg. A good husband would have literally and figuratively held me up.

Glen did not have empathy for me. Glen did not love me, hold me up, or have my back.

Chapter 20

Public vs. Private Persona

Glen had a public persona and a private persona, as is common with people who have NPD. These were very different from each other and there was an on-off switch readily accessible to him.

He would be full of charisma and the life of the party when we were at an event, but the moment the door shut to our house, he would tell me everything that I had done wrong. It was always a wide variety of missteps that I had purportedly, and unknowingly, taken. He would say the stories I had told were wrong, berate me if I didn't back up his stories to his satisfaction, express frustration that I wanted to leave too soon, etc. The list was literally endless.

He would never, ever compliment me in private. But if someone publicly praised me for something I had done, like running a marathon or publishing a scientific paper, he was full of praise for me as he basked in my sparkle as if it were his own.

He wanted to look like an important person in public, so he decided to participate in the Big Brother program. This is a great program, but when he decided to start this, time was a precious commodity. I was working full time, studying for my neurology oral boards, and taking care of an infant and a toddler. I told him the timing was not right, and I needed all the spare hours to study.

He ignored my needs. This wasn't a family discussion anyway; he was just informing me that he was doing it.

Instead of Glen taking care of our kids for a few hours each weekend, he took care of someone else's kid, and I was left to study after everyone went to bed.

But, yeah, you were a huge, important deal, Glen! Good for you!

Chapter 21

Intellect Parody

Glen would bully me by saying or texting:

"You are stupid, and you have no common sense."

"You have poor communication skills."

"You are so forgetful."

"I hate to see u always getting things wrong"

When you hear this repeatedly, it almost seems to be true. You start to believe it. I started questioning my intellect.

I would think, *I am smart enough to pass multiple exams to become a neurologist, but that was probably a fluke.* Female physicians frequently suffer from imposter syndrome, but add a narcissist into the equation, and self-doubt increases exponentially.

He knew more than me about everything, even neurology.

One time, I was speaking with the kids and explaining the importance of eating breakfast. I told them that our brain's energy source is glucose. I put it more simply by saying, "Brains run on sugar."

Glen argued, "No, the brain runs on fat."

Flabbergasted, I looked at him, "No, it runs on glucose."

"You're wrong!"

I rolled my eyes, "Okay, maybe yours uses fat then, but everyone else uses glucose."

Every once in a while, one of the kids will bring this up again, and we all laugh at the audacity of it.

Chapter 22

Why Did I Stay So Long?

When I describe my story, so many well-meaning people have said, "I would have just left!"

Oh man, that comment stings like a fastball pitch to the butt cheek!

That is a very black-and-white statement that comes from naivete as to what living with a narcissist entails.

This comment used to make me feel pathetic, weak, and foolish.

So, why did I stay? The answer is this:

I simply couldn't leave earlier. I just couldn't! The journey to that answer was complicated and convoluted, and it changed over time.

At first, I stayed because I held onto the futile hope that things would get better.

My mind swirled with such thoughts as:

Maybe I can try harder. Maybe it will be better when we are settled into our careers. Maybe it will be better once we have children.Maybe he will mature. Maybe, maybe, maybe . . .

The primary reason I stayed was our children. I was scared for their safety if they were with Glen for days at a time.

When they were young, I knew Glen was too irresponsible and distractible to take care of all their needs and keep them from harm.

He did watch them for several hours each day as a stay-at-home dad, but I wasn't certain that Glen could hold his shit together for a week at a time, or whatever amount of time the judge decided the children would be with him if we divorced.

When the kids were older, I worried about how the berating comments that Glen spewed toward them during his chaos modes would irreparably harm their psyches.

I also worried about physical abuse, because Glen was unable to dial back his rage when he spiraled. There was one chaos episode that ended with Glen punching fourteen-year-old Sawyer in the arm.

I stayed because I had no idea about our financial situation. I knew my salary, but I knew absolutely nothing else. When Glen got a job, I only knew what he said his salary was, but I never saw a pay stub or the W-2. I didn't know how much was in the checking account or savings account, as those were in his name alone. I was actively excluded from having access to the accounts. When I asked Glen to sit down and go through our finances, he would start in with gaslighting and verbal abuse.

I just couldn't voluntarily walk into that arena over and over. Once you have touched a hot stove, you do not want to put your hand back on it. I also knew there was no way in hell that Glen and I could have a meaningful conversation by that point in our relationship. It was outside of the realm of possibility.

I was so busy, working fifty to sixty hours per week, taking care of the house, and raising four kids. I was emotionally and physically exhausted just coping with things as they were. How would I find the time and energy to make a significant life change? As time went on though, I realized things were never going to change. I would keep expending all this energy, and things would never change. In fact, things were getting worse. I was doing everything, and he was making everything difficult. It was so much easier at home when he was gone, or asleep. Those brief respites were a glimpse into life after divorce.

I also waited to leave because there is shame in divorce. It is a public humiliation, despite the fact that it is so very private.

Being Catholic most of my life, I had been indoctrinated with the teaching that marriage is a sacrament and divorce is not acceptable. And if you get remarried, or have premarital relations, sit your ass on the pew during communion, as you are not welcome to partake. Just don your scarlet letter A and watch the sinless people receive communion. It is surprising how many sinless people there are though. I mean, the line was always long and included my abuser.

The topic of divorce in the Bible is interesting and full of conflicting messages. Yes, it is ideal to stay married, but abuse and infidelity are acceptable reasons for divorce.

WWJD? He would not condone financial, emotional, verbal, or physical abuse. Of this I am certain.

At every medical doctor visit and dental visit, as well as on almost every form I was going to fill out, I would be asked to choose, "married, single, widowed, or divorced." I hated when I had to pick "widowed" when I was twenty-two and I knew I would hate to pick "divorced." When I was married, I could check the "married" box and feel a sense of accomplishment. Check, I have stayed married! Even though that was not an accomplishment for me at all. It was a cop out, so I didn't have to face all the unknowns of divorce.

There are many unknowns in divorce.

Unless you are a lawyer, most people don't know the process. It is intimidating and overwhelming—almost insurmountable, really.

I didn't know how to start the process, and I was concerned that Glen would find out I was meeting with a lawyer. For my first meeting, I parked in front of a library and walked a few blocks, even though the lawyer's office was above a bank and there was no outside sign marking his office.

I didn't know where I was going to live. Would I stay in the marital home or would I be the one who moved out? If I moved out, would I ever see the inside of the house I designed, decorated, and loved? This house was full of bad memories with Glen, but it was filled with a lot of firsts and special memories with the children.

Could I risk putting my life, and our kids' lives, in the hands of the judicial system? Would I get primary physical and legal custody of the minor children?

Would I financially survive?

Would I always be alone? Alone was much better than being with Glen but I really craved love with a partner. I still really wanted the feeling of love and protection and fulfillment that I had once enjoyed with Shon.

Divorce represents failure.

I didn't want to have to admit that I was divorced. I thought I would see judging looks telling me, "Oh, yeah, she failed at marriage."

To add to my internal narrative on my failure, I had been married before. I would have had two marriages that ended, one with death and one with failure.

By nature, I am a very competitive person. I would rather dig in my heels than fail.

That seems so silly now, as divorce was not a failure at all. It was a colossal hill to climb that showed me how strong and independent I am. It was an epic success!

Divorce meant I would lose some things. Obviously, there would be a loss of the marriage, but also a loss of my routine. I would no longer come home to see my kids every day. I would possibly lose the house I thought would be my forever home. It would possibly be the loss of the backyard swimming pool I had dreamed of and worked for since high school.

Divorce means the loss of the expectation that our family would remain as a single unit.

I grew up thinking that I would get married and we would live out our lives as a cohesive unit—mother, father, and children. That would never happen and there is true grief in that!

I was recently at a wedding and sat next to a medical school classmate. He sat with his wife and two daughters. They happily whispered amongst themselves in the pew. I couldn't help but compare my fissured family to their intact family.

I just sat there and thought, "I wish I would have chosen better."

Some people, not me, even still love their abuser. I imagine that makes the prospect of leaving more difficult as well, because it would mean heartbreak.

I also stayed because of the trauma bond I had with my abuser. I'll delve into this topic in the next chapter.

So, I didn't leave until I could. When I was ready. When I felt my kids were ready. When the benefits appeared to outweigh the risks. When I knew my soul would die if I stayed any longer.

After all this happened, I left the son-of-a-bitch.

Chapter 23

I Needed to Run

While I was biding my time, obligated to remain in a loveless and abusive marriage, I started to run regularly at age forty. The hypnotic sound of my shoes on the gravel roads near our home became my therapy. I used this time to sort my thoughts. To remember who I was. To pray. To save myself.

I started by running two miles a few times per week and slowly increased my mileage. With the constant gaslighting, and the fact that I had not yet discovered the importance of professional therapy, the miles added up. Soon, I was running marathons.

When I had frustrating interactions with Glen, my body would feel jittery, and I just felt like I needed to go for a run. Running briefly helped release this energy.

After my runs, I would frequently not recall several of the miles. I attributed this to a "runner's high" from natural endorphins, but I think it was more that my brain was so consumed with working through what had happened, what my life had become, and what I should have as a plan, that my mind just never registered the miles.

There is so much good that came from exercising for me. Besides the therapy and the obvious health benefits, it became time spent with each of my children individually. As they got old enough, they would run with me or bike beside me as I ran. This was quality time as they discussed what was going on in school and occasionally what their dreams were for their future. This was also when I would learn about friend drama that we had the time to sort out or put into perspective.

Charles, who would become an excellent long-distance runner in high school, serendipitously learned to control his pace and breathing as he told me long stories about Greek mythology. At the same time, I learned patience, and the importance of a well-timed nod of the head or "mmm-hmmm." Greek mythology is interesting, and I was amazed at the amount of factual knowledge in this kid's brain.

I ran four marathons, in addition to several 5Ks, 10Ks, ten-mile races, and half marathons. I did a few triathlons during those years and continue those today. Exercise remains an important form of therapy for me, but I also reap the benefits of professional therapy.

Chapter 24

Marriage Counseling

We attempted marriage counseling. Oddly, it was by Glen's insistence that this was even scheduled. Why? I honestly don't know.

By this point, we had been married for about eighteen years and the kids ranged from age seven to fifteen. I was mentally done with the marriage and was just biding my time. I was waiting for the kids to get a little older and for Glen to get back to work so he wasn't inappropriately labeled as the primary caregiver per the hobbled and archaic court system.

I suspect Glen scheduled therapy because he knew I was done and this was simply smoke and mirrors, appearing as if he was working at the relationship. Maybe he had met with a lawyer, and they had suggested this for appearance as well.

At the time of this therapy, I was naive to Glen's diagnosis and to what constitutes gaslighting. I had never even heard that word. I just didn't know what was happening to my life. In medical school and residency, I had learned the basics of narcissism, but at that time I was reading to learn to treat patients, not to survive my own relationship.

Over the past several years, I have read, researched, listened to podcasts, and gotten appropriate therapy with a therapist who is knowledgeable in NPD and trauma. I have educated myself and now I know, without a doubt, what Glen is and that I was a victim who was trauma bonded.

Unfortunately, despite several sessions, our marriage counselor was inept. She failed to make the diagnosis of NPD and was therefore unable to help.

I needed a therapist with experience and interest in NPD and trauma. I didn't know those were the issues that were killing my soul. It was her job to sort this out and she didn't.

She failed to see beyond Glen's charisma. She would laugh and get sidetracked, by his dumb jokes during sessions. These were usually jokes at my expense.

After several sessions, I lost hope. This was going nowhere. If a professional in mental health couldn't help, then who could? I was overwhelmed with my feeling of helplessness.

I am very verbal and expressive, and I was desperate for help, so I was giving it my all. She failed me!

The sessions also fine-tuned his abuse.

The therapist would ask detailed questions about the feelings we experienced during an argument.

I would answer seriously and with great thought. Glen

continued to joke around and didn't take any of it seriously.

During the sessions, I would tell him what really hurt me. He would then use this to cut right to my heart during an argument.

And Glen told the therapist I had rage issues.

Anyone who has been part of a gaslighting incident understands how incredibly frustrating they are. At home, Glen would make a false statement and then walk away when I started to talk. I would then respond with rightful anger.

The therapist told him that if I got mad, he should say, "I am going to walk away for a few minutes and come back once we have calmed down."

The therapist simply gave him a reason to do what he was already doing, walking away like the coward he was. He did not, however, come back, or even plan to come back, to finish the discussion. Once he said what he wanted, he was done with the conversation.

Even as I write this, I can feel the anger that I had felt during those moments. It was the rightful anger of being attacked yet castrated of any ability to respond.

The therapist did tell him that I would leave if he didn't get a job, so that was one thing that was true and that I was glad she told him. One tiny gem obtained from several frustrating and fruitless sessions. I expected more. I deserved more.

Chapter 25

Infidelity

I was starting to suspect that Glen was having an affair. Initially I didn't have hard facts, just my intuition. But I started to notice very subtle things.

I am very compulsive in how I make beds. As a nurses' aide in high school and college, I was taught to make "hospital corners" by an old Army nurse. I have continued with this method of bed-making ever since. Well, a couple times I noticed that our bed had been made differently, not the haphazard way Glen would do it, but not the way I did it either. The second time I noted this, Glen was in the room. I pointed out the difference.

"Are you having an affair?" I asked.

He simply walked out of the room. There was no further discussion on this matter because he was done with it.

Certainly, someone wrongly accused would get angry, yet a guilty man would avoid the discussion.

I knew I could trust my intuition.

Another time, Glen returned from a work trip after being gone for a few days. He made a few trips from the garage as he brought his things into the house. I was doing laundry and walking back and forth past the door to the garage. On one of my trips back to the laundry room, I saw a pair of hot pink G-string panties on the floor. These skanky panties had not been there a few minutes prior. I got a grocery bag and picked them up without allowing them to touch my hand. They were not mine and there was a long blonde hair wrapped around one side of the panties. I have dark brown hair, as does my daughter. Molly was home from college, so I asked if they were hers or maybe one of friends. They were not.

I had the opportunity to discuss another incident in detail with my mother shortly before she died. We were in her hospital room, and she awoke to my typing of this memoir. She asked me to read her some of this book. I read her several parts, but there was one story that she was able to add more clarity to.

My mother lived about five hours from us. One day, Glen and Hunter, age eleven, were near her home, staying with a friend, so they met her for supper at a bar and grill.

Here is what she described:

> I was standing at the bar, talking to Alice (an acquaintance), when another lady started to quickly walk past us, toward where Glen stood. Alice reached out and grabbed the other woman's arm, eyes locked on where Glen stood. Alice said,

"This is Glen's mother-in-law," putting forceful emphasis on each word.

This was odd, as I already knew both women. No introduction was necessary.

My gut told me something was up.

I sat my beer on the counter, said goodbye to Hunter, and left. I talked to Kay (my sister), about this interaction, as I was not sure if I should tell you. Kay said you needed to be told.

I fretted for a couple days before I called you to tell you that I suspected Glen was having an affair.

When I recall this interaction, the telling of her thought process, I felt the struggle in her heart as she wanted to protect me by telling me what she suspected, but she wanted to avoid hurting me if it was not an accurate assessment of the situation. At the point when this story took place, I was not sharing my marital issues with many friends or family, so she did not know how close I was to jumping off the cliff into divorce. But she chose to have my back. I also recall how much we laughed as she recalled this story, laughing at the idiocy and shenanigans that were a part of who Glen is. We were both glad I was out of the marriage.

Chapter 26

Why Did He Develop NPD?

My answer to this question is an opinion, as I am not a psychiatrist or psychologist. I believe many factors were involved.

Glen's father was a chronic alcoholic. He finally went to alcohol rehabilitation in 2003, but prior to that, he always had a Jim Beam in his hand, or within close reach. He even had a drink in a thermal cup as he got out of the car for the baptism of one of his grandchildren. Fortunately, his wife was driving that day.

Somehow, his children were all blind to the fact that he was an alcoholic. Glen was shocked when I insisted that he stop dropping our toddler and infant off for his father to babysit, while he did whatever the hell he was doing as a stay-at-home dad. I was furious to hear his father had taken the kids for a ride in his car. My PTSD was flaring. Not only had my first husband died in a car accident, but it was at the hands of a drinking driver.

"You're crazy," Glen said. "You're overreacting. My dad is fine."

About two years later, we were at a birthday party for one of our nephews. I was in the kitchen when someone yelled, "Call 911!"

I rushed into the living room to find my father-in-law unconscious on the floor.

I knelt beside him and felt for a pulse. None!

I put my cheek down by his mouth to feel for air movement. None! Crap!

Just as I positioned myself to start CPR, he gasped and opened his eyes.

He tried to sit up and I told him to stay down as I was sure his blood pressure was low as I had not been able to feel a pulse seconds before.

The ambulance arrived and the Emergency Medical Technician (EMT) checked his blood pressure, which was alarmingly low. My father-in-law refused to allow the EMTs to take him to the hospital.

Glen's mother drove him to the emergency department a couple hours later, and he was admitted to the hospital. She then refused to take him home until he completed an inpatient alcohol rehabilitation program, as was recommended by the physician caring for him.

My mother-in-law told all her eight children that she couldn't afford rehab, so she needed their help.

Glen told me this and I said we needed to decide together

how much we could financially contribute. I was working and Glen was not, so obviously the money was coming from me. Glen paid an amount that was never disclosed to me, despite my pleas.

Glen liked to be the Big Man on Campus with my earnings, so I am certain I funded most of it. Alcohol had killed my first husband and now I was paying again, in a different way. The irony!

My father-in-law was frequently sexually inappropriate with me and the other five sisters-in-law. I would act like I had not heard him or I would simply look away and ignore him. Glen never protected me from this, even though I privately told him, many times, this made me uncomfortable.

Glen would roll his eyes at me and say, "It is a joke."

Okay! I thought. *Yes, you're right, I am the problem. It is me. I am a stick-in-the-mud and it is not possibly your seventy-five-year-old father who is the problem.*

One example of this, among many, would occur just after anyone announced their pregnancy. He would say, "You know the gender of the baby is decided by whose idea it was." This was said with a knowing grin and a raising of his eyebrows.

To be fair to him, despite these two character flaws, he was otherwise a good person. He was a joyful man, and I never recall him speaking poorly about anyone.

Glen's mother was not very nurturing. She wasn't mean, just not outwardly loving or affectionate.

I don't feel Glen, as the sixth child, was raised in a way that encouraged him to mature with a fully developed, emotionally intelligent personality. He just had a poor foundation for emotional growth.

Glen was raised in a family in which there was a culture of lying and embellishment. It was a joke amongst the in-laws that everything stated by this family needed to be divided by a factor of three.

Some of the family members were worse than others, and Glen was the master of this skill.

I didn't witness how Glen was raised, as I had met him in college, but I did hear a lot of stories and observed the family dynamics for more than two decades.

My perception is that there were just too many children for this particular family to raise and adequately nurture. As a result, Glen and his siblings have persistent attention-seeking behaviors. They speak loudly and all talk over each other as if they are in a competition for the best story. It is exhausting to witness. And it is very much a stimulation overload.

NPD is complex for sure, but I think these environmental factors clinched the disorder in someone whose brain was already predisposed.

Chapter 27

Chosen One

People with NPD are drawn to partners with certain characteristics, which is why I was Glen's chosen one.

I am a strong, confident, and self-assured woman. These are characteristics narcissists prey upon, but not the characteristics I would have previously thought would make me prone to victimization.

People with NPD subconsciously seek people with these traits as this provides external validation that they themselves are worthy. This is inherently what they are drawn to.

But why didn't I see that Glen was a narcissist before we married? There are several answers to this question. First of all, Glen did not have all his traits fully developed when we met. Everything was more subtle and insidiously became more pronounced. Additionally, I was young and still believed people had the best intentions until they showed me otherwise, which he eventually did. And I think most importantly, I was traumatized by the death of my husband. I wanted love back. I wanted companionship back. I wanted what I had lost. I wanted this to the degree that I had blinders for potential red flags.

Chapter 28

Trauma Bond

The trauma bond is a deep, unhealthy, emotional attachment that a victim feels for their abuser.

Here's how it develops: during a threatening situation, the victim seeks protection—and the only person available is the abuser.

Glen was my husband, my theoretical protector who was supposed to have my back. It was natural for me to turn to him for help when I felt threatened.

But as the victim reaches for help from the abuser, they become more and more entangled with them.

The trauma bond is hard to fathom until you understand the biology behind this bond. This is based on survival instinct, not logic. The neurobiology explains why rational people fall prey to, and remain subject to, people with NPD.

Trauma bonding with a narcissist has seven stages:
- love-bombing;
- trust and dependency;
- criticism;
- manipulation;
- giving up control;
- losing yourself; and
- addiction to the cycle.

In retrospect, I went through all these stages. At the time though, I was simply surviving and did not have the insight to see what was happening.

"Love-bombing" is when the abuser showers you with loving words and gestures. It seems as if you were made for each other, when in actuality the abuser is simply contorting to your likes and dislikes to seem as if you are the same person.

We seemed, on first blush, to be very aligned. We both felt family was important. We both loved the outdoors. We were both in school and had career goals. We had grown up in the same religion.

These seemed like important commonalities, but his actions were not matching up.

For example, my love of the outdoors meant hiking, biking, swimming, and simply breathing in the fresh air. His love of the outdoors meant hunting.

Another example involved our career goals. We both had stated goals, mine to be a medical doctor and his to be a high school teacher and coach. But actions speak louder than words. So much louder!

I was diligently marching toward my career. Glen, on the

other hand, attended college for seven years before having enough credits for a bachelor's degree, and that was without completing his student teaching. No student teaching means no teaching.

I don't remember much love-bombing from Glen, other than the presumed commonalities described.

Maybe the love bomb phase was fleeting, so I forgot it.

Maybe, on a subconscious level, I did not feel it was genuine, so I forgot it.

More likely, my favorite organ—the brain—was protecting me from pain and trauma, so I forgot it.

The "trust and dependency" phase in the trauma bond is where the victim begins to trust the abuser's level of dedication to them. The victim then begins to depend on their validation for their own self-worth. This is an unhealthy dependency.

I trusted that Glen had my best interest at heart and that he was dedicated to me.

Was this something Glen made me feel or was it a theoretical cultural expectation? I think it was a bit of both.

I did feel that my self-worth, or lack thereof, came from Glen's words.

When he said I was stupid, I thought, *He knows me best, so I guess that is true.* Because, what in the hell does the American Academy of Neurology know, right?

"Criticism" is the stage in which the narcissist blames you for things that you have no control over.

This stage started early and was pervasive throughout our relationship. Glen was good at this one and below are several examples.

During a drive home from church, Glen was lecturing new driver Molly about how she had run over a small scooter in our driveway while backing up the Suburban. He was telling her that she needed to pay better attention to her surroundings. Unfortunately, he did not use this parenting moment in an effective way, but rather used it as an opportunity to berate her.

He repeatedly called her, "Scooter Killer."

As he continued to taunt her, he pulled into the garage and shut the garage door.

He then, unexpectedly, put the vehicle into reverse and backed up into the closed garage door.

He immediately turned to me and blamed me!

Somehow, I drove the car into the garage from the passenger seat. How, you ask? Nobody knows! This is just one of the illogical scenarios that happened with absolutely no way to understand his thought process.

We barely made it behind closed doors before Molly and I were bent over laughing at the irony of the situation. The "Scooter Killer" Molly then secretly pronounced that Glen was "Garage Door Killer."

As our belly laughter eased, I realized I was the one who would be paying for that damage because he was not working.

Of course, Glen was not at fault when two minor car accidents happened while he was driving.

One occurred while we were dating, when he rear-ended someone at a stop sign. He immediately blamed me, because we were arguing when he did it. He then said the other driver should have seen him coming and turned faster.

The other event occurred when he was backing up in the

grocery store parking lot and hit another car.

Somehow, from the passenger side, these were all my fault. I apparently have a very strange, and useless, superpower.

"Manipulation" is another stage in trauma bonding. Abusers with NPD often use this very harmful form of emotional abuse in the form of gaslighting.

The victim eventually gives up control, as they attempt to change their personality and everything that makes them who they are, in a futile attempt to get back to the love-bombing phase.

This makes me so sad because I did this! I attempted to contort to what I thought Glen wanted me to be. I was changing who I was made to be.

Sadly, you eventually lose yourself and resign yourself to the abuse. You choose misery because you can't see a way out and because you are addicted to the repetitive cycle of abuse and positive reinforcement. By this stage, you cannot even find the person you were before the first stage of this trauma bonding cycle began.

I recall wondering, *Who am I? I don't even like the person I have become.* This was a very grievous place to be.

The trauma bond forms from the repeating cycle of torment and a loving reward.

My life was this cycle. My abuser would gaslight me and then follow intermittently and randomly with positive reinforcement. The positive reinforcement posed as acts of love, such as telling me he loved me or giving me shower gel and chocolate. Actually, shower gel and chocolate were his go-to gifts for every single Christmas and Mother's Day. I mean every single one! He could have at least used two brain cells and a synapse twice per year to be more creative. But alas . . . that was not possible!

Since the rewards from a narcissist are random and intermittent, the feeling is very similar to a gambling addiction. You never know when the reward will come, so you keep trying and hoping it will come with the next day or next card game.

Once you are trauma bonded, the abuser can lie, cheat, and generally be a toxic person, but you will stay put in the relationship. You will endure incredible toxicity. They have you right where they wanted you all along.

I was in this phase for a very, very long time.

A trauma bond with a narcissist develops through intense, repeated emotional cycles that hijack the limbic system—the part of the brain that governs emotion, memory, and survival instincts. This neurological entanglement makes it extremely difficult for victims to leave the relationship, even when they know it's unhealthy.

Therefore, it was biology, neurobiology specifically, that made me stay! The irony is not lost on me that my favorite organ, the brain, was the one trapping me in an abusive relationship.

My situation was not my fault, but I did eventually leave by my own choice—a well-calculated and well-timed choice. I left and initiated the gradual, progressive weakening of the trauma bond, as that rope began to fray, string by string.

Chapter 29

The Limbic System

Dr. Pierre Paul Broca was a French surgeon and anthropologist in the 1800s. He called the limbic system the *"grand lobe limbique."* I love this! It sounds complicated and important and tragic and lovely and mysterious, all of which the limbic system is.

The limbic system is incredibly complex and, I will admit, I had to get out my old neuroanatomy book and notes for a refresher.

The limbic system is responsible for our fight, flight, or freeze response. This response is our most basic survival mechanism. But it is much more than that. It is responsible for the emotions that are important for our own survival and for the survival of our species, such as fear and sexual excitement. It is responsible for our defensive reactions, such as rage and aggression. It provides the visceral (gut) responses to our emotions and is part of a complex system for housing our memory.

The limbic system has strong connections with the prefrontal cortex and anterior temporal lobes, which are the brain regions responsible for memory, motivation, judgment, and emotion.

This part of the brain responds automatically and rapidly when we encounter a threat, or even something that reminds us of a prior threat. This is protective when the only goal at that moment is to get you away from the threat. A threat—or even the memory of one—activates a visceral, "gut-level" response as the body instinctively shifts into fight, flight, or freeze mode.

The activation of the limbic system, and the release of stress hormones, disables the higher functioning prefrontal cortex, slowing its response. So, the very portion of the brain, the prefrontal cortex, that can provide reasoning around the danger, is slowed. Once the prefrontal cortex re-engages, you can draw on past experiences and use insight and reasoning to accurately assess the level of threat and choose an appropriate response.

Think of my response to flashing lights, as this is a perfect example of limbic system activation. I immediately perceive a threat and have a guttural response. Soon thereafter, my prefrontal cortex activates, and I can think rationally that this is a memory and not a current threat. A more ubiquitous example is when you reflexively hit the brakes when you see a highway patrol, even if you aren't speeding. Only after you hit the brakes, and feel the guttural response, or butterflies, do you use the executive portion of your brain to realize you are not speeding and have done nothing wrong, or that you are actually speeding and will probably get pulled over for a ticket.

I mentioned that the limbic system is where the fight, flight, or freeze response occurs when someone is threatened. My personal response is to fight. When verbally attacked by Glen, I would verbally mount a counterattack. An emotionally draining, and unfruitful, battle would ensue as I attempted to use verbal reasoning to defend myself. Glen would then double down his verbal attack, further activating my limbic system and deactivating my frontal lobes. It was a never-ending and impossible battle.

When I occasionally responded with flight, Glen would pursue me and continue his verbal assault.

My personal limbic response is not typically to freeze. If this is your response though, the freeze response will immobilize you, cause you to relent and just take the blame. However, this ultimately results in further criticism by a person with NPD as they berate you for being weak.

Chapter 30

Post Traumatic Stress Disorder (PTSD)

PTSD is when the mind and body continue to fight a threat that is no longer present. Post Traumatic Stress Disorder happens after you lived through something awful, and your brain stored that information incorrectly, basically without filing it away as a past event. Therefore, when you are triggered, you feel like it is a danger that is happening right now.

I have PTSD triggered by red flashing lights, as well as several triggers that Glen placed in my path. They are my landmines, and they are tricky fuckers to avoid.

It has been decades since the car accident, yet flashing red lights instantly put me back in the ditch. It is as if time stopped with the crash and my brain continues to respond as if there is a current threat. My stomach drops, adrenaline surges, and I need to contact any loved ones that could potentially be in the vicinity of the lights. I worry until I verify each person's safety.

Even now, if an unexpected call comes from my kids, no matter the time of day, I instantly worry. I listen to their tone and the first few words to decide if they are delivering bad news. Once I know they are not, I can settle into the conversation.

On one specific occasion, my son-in-law called at 12:30 a.m. He started the conversation with, "Molly is fine, but . . . " I have thanked him for this approach many times since that day. When he called, I could hear the noise of a paramedic's walkie talkie, so my trauma brain immediately deduced that she had been in a car accident. Fortunately, she had only fainted in a restaurant due to jetlag.

Meanwhile, my PTSD from Glen comes in many flavors.

I am triggered whenever I encounter a narcissist, even if I have not yet identified them as such. My gut knows before my brain knows. I am triggered when I need to repurchase something that I previously bought, but it is at the prior marital home where Glen now resides. Something I paid for but was forced to give to my abuser. I am triggered when I need to ask my financial planner to move money to my checking account, as this feels like I am asking for my own money. This trigger will be explained in detail later, but basically, I had to ask Glen to give me money whenever I needed it. I am triggered when I can hear Glen's voice while my kids are talking to him on the phone near me. I am triggered when the kids talk about the pool. Plus, so many, many more.

I call the prior marital home "The House I Paid For" throughout this book. I call it this because I was the only one who worked for eleven of the fifteen years that I lived there. This has nothing to do with the final divorce settlement that will not be discussed in this book. It is simply something that feels better for my financially abused brain.

Frustrated with all these triggers, I sought to understand why my brain and mind were making me relive the trauma over and over. I found the fascinating answer in the book, *The Body Keeps the Score: Brain, Mind, and Body in the Healing of Trauma* by Bessel van der Kolk, M.D.

Dr. van der Kolk, and his team used PET (positron emission tomography) scanners to see which areas of the brain were activated or inactivated in response to study subjects who were reading scripts of their personal traumatic event. PET scanners measure metabolism in the brain, as opposed to CT (computed tomography) or MRI (magnetic resonance imaging) scans that show anatomy.

In their study, PET scans revealed that the limbic system became activated, which is not surprising given the role of the limbic system as it prepares for fight or flight. They also found that metabolism decreased in one of the speech areas (known as Broca's Area) in the left frontal lobe. There are different areas of the brain for different parts of speech. Wernicke's area is for understanding what is spoken or written, while Broca's Area formulates words and allows you to physically speak. With Broca's Area showing a decrease in function, this explains why you can be literally speechless when trauma occurs, or PTSD is activated.

Particularly interesting for me was that Brodman's Area 19, in the visual cortex—which plays a critical role in processing visual information—became activated on the PET scans as subjects read their script. During normal situations that are not traumatic, images enter Brodman's Area 19 and are rapidly redistributed to other areas of the brain to interpret their meaning. They are filed in the correct, innocuous file.

But with trauma, the images remain stuck in Brodman's Area 19 and can be reactivated with PTSD, with flashing lights in my case. To the traumatized person, it feels as if the trauma is occurring again. Right now. Time does not, in fact, heal your trauma on its own. Time helps soften your response, but it takes intentional work, often with a therapist, to understand why the symptoms are happening and to learn how to decrease the impact that these symptoms have on your overall functioning.

We use both sides of our brain all the time, but in general the right brain is creative, emotional, and intuitive while the left is verbal, logical, analytical, and detail oriented. The right side of our brain controls the left side of our body and vice versa for the left side of our brain. I am right-handed and fit the classic description of a left-brained person. However, cursing is right brained, so I know that side works well!

Flashbacks are a common symptom of PTSD. Dr. van der Kolk's research shows that during a flashback—or when viewing trauma-related images—the right hemisphere of the brain becomes highly activated, while the left hemisphere becomes deactivated. In short, the emotional side of your brain is activated, and the logical, factual, sequencing side is shut down. This imbalance causes you to relive the trauma as if it's happening in the present moment.

As I noted earlier, at the scene of the accident where Shon died, I was unable to stop crying. I was physically unable to stop. Crying is nonverbal and that activity comes from the right brain, the emotional side. Since my left brain was essentially turned off during the acute trauma, I would not use logic to stop my crying.

In addition to the imbalance between the two halves of our brains, the prefrontal cortex slows down under extreme stress when the limbic system takes over. This makes it even harder to assess and process a perceived or remembered threat. Eventually, the left brain and prefrontal cortex "come back online," allowing logic and reasoning to re-engage.

Our stressed brains are trying so hard, but this is an uphill battle for sure. People can live in this state for months or years, which makes therapeutic intervention even more important and challenging, as this becomes our brain's "normal."

Adrenaline, also known as epinephrine, is a hormone and neurotransmitter that is part of our body's response to stress or danger. It is released from our brain and adrenal glands when our fight or flight response is activated. Adrenaline is less regulated in traumatized people. It spikes higher and takes longer to come back down to its normal baseline, so it takes longer to recover from even mildly stressful events. Adrenaline increases our blood pressure, breathing rate, and heart rate, often producing a panicky, out-of-control sensation.

If you have to suppress your fight or flight response to survive, such as when you are physically or emotionally trapped in an abusive relationship, your adrenaline is released but it hits a roadblock in your brain, and your body is unable to respond.

This is not good for our overall health, particularly when it is long lasting, and several chronic illnesses have been linked to chronic stress.

This information explains my desire to run when my limbic system is activated, even if there is not a physical threat that requires me to run away. I have found that going for a run just makes me feel better. I have to run it out. Some people run for the adrenaline high, but these necessary runs are to bring my adrenaline back into check.

My trauma and PTSD cause other issues as well. Happiness frightens me, as I know it can be gone in an instant. If I am happy with everything in my life, this triggers a feeling that the other shoe will drop. If everything is going well, I feel this is a phase that can't be maintained. Life can change quickly. That is the deal.

I am working hard on my PTSD symptoms, but it is a work in progress. My therapist has taught me how to use visualization when I am triggered. I visualize my younger self standing in a thunderstorm, frozen in place with a look of bewilderment and fear. I put my motherly arms around this younger version of myself and walk her into the sunshine. I let her know that I am with her and will protect her. I also let her know that I value her for making me who I am—strong, empowered, empathetic, and compassionate.

Chapter 31

Was I in a State of Depression?

In the movie *Gaslight,* Paula expresses a pronounced state of depression.

During my marriage to Glen, I felt frustrated and trapped, but was I depressed?

I felt sad for what my life had become, or actually what it had not become. I felt hopeless in finding a way to get out of the marriage without hurting my children. I lost weight during the first stages of the divorce, as I had absolutely no appetite. Honestly, if I thought of the sadness of my situation while I was eating, I found it hard to physically swallow.

I was agitated and felt on edge, a sign that my limbic system was constantly stuck in the "on position." I also felt guilty that my kids were dealing with a dysfunctional household.

However, I did not lose interest in activities, have sleep issues or experience fatigue. I did not have particular difficulty concentrating or have recurrent thoughts of death or suicidal ideation. So, I didn't meet enough of these criteria for a diagnosis of depression, but I was close. My mental health was clearly being impacted.

Unlike Paula, I had a job. My job provided our income and social status, which is important to people with NPD. That job was also the reason I had the ability to leave the marriage and still financially provide for myself and my children.

My job also provided me with a built-in social network. In fact, a fellow neurologist, Jenny, was my unwavering source of support. She offered a safe space place to vent and a non-judgmental platform upon which I could describe what was happening to me.

Work was also a place I enjoyed being. I love practicing neurology, and I loved being with people that I genuinely enjoyed. It was a constant and reliable source of joy that I needed.

It was also helpful that I had proven my intellect despite Glen telling me that I was stupid and had no common sense. I had proof that I was intelligent from my undergraduate university, my medical school, my residency program, and the American Board of Psychiatry and Neurology. I had taken thousands of exams, whose sole purpose was to ensure that I mastered the material. I had passed multiple board exams, culminating in my specialty exams. I had passed them all.

When Glen told me I was stupid or that I recalled our conversations incorrectly, I would briefly believe him. However, after my limbic system would calm down, my prefrontal cortex would kick in and I could think rationally. I would remember that I had several academic achievements that were in direct contrast to Glen's statements. I knew I was smart, and that I was recalling events correctly.

This was a Glen issue, not a me issue. The Rat Bastard!

☙

As I described, exercise was essential for me during my marriage. After I started the divorce process, I started therapy. These were both instrumental in my journey to emotional wellness. I have always been active, but running and swimming became more regular and systematic as my life became more chaotic.

When my father died, I used part of my inheritance to buy a Bianchi road bike and added cycling to my routine. Buying and riding this bike was special and freeing, because it was from my dad and because I had access to my own money with that inheritance.

When I started exercising regularly during my marriage, I knew it made me feel better—and during those dark years, anything that offered even the slightest relief was something I clung to. While I expected physical benefits, I was surprised by how much better my mind began to feel. Exercise became an outlet for my overactive limbic system, which was flooding my body with cortisol. Activities like running, biking, and swimming helped burn off that stress hormone while also giving me quiet, meditative time to process and organize my thoughts.

In short, I was protected from some of the depressive symptoms by many different factors. This included my family and social network, exercise, and my ability to financially provide for my family.

☙

Living with someone who has NPD is very difficult. It is hard to relax as you are constantly pushed to conform to the narcissist's current needs, wants, and demands. These needs, wants, and demands are often a mystery to the victim as they are exclusively housed in the abuser's brain.

The constant verbal abuse eroded my self-esteem, just as dripping water eventually erodes stone. It takes months or years, but it happens.

I feel lucky that I had the components in place to keep me mentally strong. I still needed therapy to live my best life, but I was able to weather the storm and get out.

Chapter 32

Financial Abuse

It's difficult for me to reflect on this part of my journey, because I experienced severe financial abuse—and honestly, it's embarrassing.

I kept asking myself, *how did I let this happen?*

The truth is, it was easier than I ever imagined. People with narcissistic personality disorder are masters of manipulation. Their actions are driven by self-preservation, not by what's best for the relationship or the family.

Financial abuse is a form of control where one person manipulates or restricts another's access to money, assets, or financial resources to gain power and control over them. It can happen in romantic relationships, families, or care-giver situations.

It's basically the inability to control your own finances. This definition is short and concise.

But in reality, financial abuse is so complex and so frustrating and so disheartening and so disabling and so immobilizing, that it is hard to put into words that do it justice. Financial abuse is the complete gutting of your independence.

I had an education and thriving career. This gave me the ability to provide for myself and my family, and it should have enabled me to create a comfortable and stable life. However, this ability was stolen from me. Stolen by my poor choice of a mate. Stolen by a bad person. Stolen and locked down with the code hidden deep in a very sick brain.

I had zero control over my finances for the entirety of my marriage. This was one of the myriad ways Glen maintained control over me. How could I leave? I had no idea what our financial situation was, and Glen was unwilling to share this information. In fact, he very intentionally hid it from me.

The financial abuse started insidiously, but it was very systematic. Glen had an agenda as he skillfully lied and manipulated to meet his goal. People with NPD must control the money. They must.

Here's how he did it.

One month after we got married, I started residency. The term "residency" has recently lost its original meaning as several medical professionals, other than doctors, have started to use this term to signify any additional learning, or even classes, after graduation. The original meaning arises from the fact that medical residents actually lived at the hospital or spent the majority of their life there for the three to seven years of their medical residency program. This is what I was doing. I was working eighty to 100 hours in the hospital or clinic and that work was intense.

During this time, Glen said he should manage the budget, and I thought that would be fine, as I was having a hard time finding time to shower, eat, and sleep, let alone pay bills. He later doubled down and said it would just be easier if all our money went into one checking account—his, of course—and then he could pay bills from it. This seemed reasonable enough. A few months later, he dug the hole even deeper and said that my name should not be on the checking account, as it was five dollars extra each month. That is such a moronic statement, and it would be laughable if it wasn't actually tragic. This was the start of his gaslighting.

Every couple weeks, I would ask Glen for cash. Yes, I had to ask! He would give me the amount he felt was needed, after grilling me on what I had spent my prior "allowance" on.

I recall one embarrassing incident in which he went out of state for work when Molly was an infant. He was supposed to be gone for one week, but this turned into three weeks. I ran out of cash and had no access to our money. This was before the days of easy cash transfers through apps, and before I had a credit card.

Glen sent one of his friends to our house to give me cash. I felt so humiliated! After that happened, I told him the checking needed to be a joint account. He said it couldn't because we might both write a check the same day and that might cause an overdraft charge. Yes, there are several logical responses to that statement, but he would agree to none of that. By this relatively early point in our marriage, it was already becoming easier to play along with him than to argue. I just relented and convinced myself that I should trust my husband.

Several years later, I joined the local fitness club.

Glen told the kids, "We need to cut back because mom joined the Wellness Center." My kids recall him sitting them all down in the living room to tell them this information.

The cost was sixty dollars per month for a family pass in 2006. We should have been able to afford that for cripes' sakes!

When the kids told me this, my heart raced. My limbic system activated. But why?

My logical brain started to try to figure this out. The problem inherent in logical thinking, when dealing with NPD, is that they do not think logically. They always approach things in a manner that fulfills their own agenda.

Are we so short of money that we can't afford the membership? I wondered. *He knows the financial situation so that may be the case,* I reasoned. *Or . . . did he say this because he was controlling me and the money?*

❧

One weekend day several years later, I looked outside and saw Glen riding a new lawnmower. The huge, top-of-the-line, expensive, zero-turn kind of lawn mower. This had not been discussed or even mentioned to me. We already had two working mowers, so I went outside, waited for Glen to stop the mower, and asked, "Why do we have a new mower?"

He said, "We needed it." He turned the mower back on, drowning out my response, and drove away. Glen always had to have the best of everything.

When I discussed this with my father, he dryly said, "Only the best for Glen."

Only the best because he had a sense of entitlement and a lack of self-control, both typical of NPD. Addictive spending was also one of his self-soothing behaviors.

Glen had the sense that he could have whatever he wanted, whenever he wanted it. Unfortunately, my long work hours were funding this behavior.

After I filed for divorce, I learned that when people in our small town saw Glen with something new, they would shrug and say, "The life of Glen." At first this made me chuckle, but on further introspection, I felt like a chump.

❦

Another time, I wanted to update our kitchen, so I priced out granite countertops. I presented this proposal to Glen, as I started my campaign to get something I wanted.

In the kids' presence, Glen said, "We can't afford granite countertops because we have four kids." This was shortly after Hunter was born.

The kids then nick-named their youngest sibling, "Granite Countertops." It is funny now, but the kids and I all knew the countertops would not be replaced. The House That I Paid For still has laminate countertops that are more than twenty-six years old.

❦

One day, Glen called me at work from the car dealership.

He informed me that he was getting approved for a pickup loan. This was the first time I heard of a new pickup purchase, and I was busy in the middle of a full patient load in the clinic. He was well aware that I didn't have time for a long discussion.

I said, "I don't think we have enough money."

He responded, "I take care of the finances, and we can afford it."

He hung up. End of discussion.

To put the extravagance of this into perspective, this was now our sixth vehicle in a family with five drivers. We also already owned a pickup, and he did not trade this in for the new pickup, he was keeping that as well. Meanwhile, I drove a diesel, manual Jetta.

After the divorce, I was looking for a car for Hunter.

I asked the dealer, "What is the cheapest car on the lot?"

His response, "The manual, diesel Jetta."

"Of course, it is," I chuckled.

When I would need a new car, about every eight years, I would tell Glen I wanted a VW Beetle. He would then go to the Volkswagen dealership and buy another Jetta for me.

I was making a great income, but all I could ever get, for myself, was the cheapest car on the lot, while he drove a fully loaded pickup truck. Only the best for Glen.

☙

Another time, Glen called me, again while I was busy at work, and said, "I am on my way to look at a trailer that a guy has for sale."

I expressed my concern for the spending that was occurring. He simply responded that he needed it. I am not sure why we needed it, as we already had a trailer. Again, he was not trading in the old trailer, just adding a new one to our fleet.

I later learned that this was a dealership selling a new trailer, not a person selling a used trailer. I discovered this when I saw Hunter wearing a hat from the dealership and asked him where he got it. He told me Glen bought it for him at the dealership where he bought the trailer.

❧

In August 2014, I received a call from my business accountant. She said my check needed to be mailed to me, as Glen's checking account had been closed.

I had no idea what this was about, as it involved finances and was therefore deliberately kept from me.

I called Glen, who finally had a job, and told him about the account issues.

He said, "I am going into a meeting at work right now, I will call you back." Ten minutes later, he called me from the bank to ask what the accountant had told me.

Glen had trouble keeping track of all his lies, so of course he did not even attempt to explain how he could have completed a meeting, driven to the bank, and spoken with a banker already.

He said, "I took care of the problem."

"What was the problem?" I asked, genuinely interested in what had happened.

"I am with the banker. I will tell you later." Glen hung up.

When I asked him later that evening, he said, "Why are you accusing me of closing the account? You yelled at me over speaker phone while I was with the banker. He rolled his eyes when you were yelling."

It was common for Glen to confabulate stories that made it seem as if I was the crazy person. I had not yelled at all. This tactic also took me off guard and distracted me briefly from the actual topic at hand.

Glen never did tell me what happened. He gave me a new checking account number, again with just his name on it. By this point, I was even more unsettled than usual. I asked Glen to show me the checking account, so I could see what our overall financial situation was. He wouldn't show me.

I told him I was going to go to the bank to see if they could enlighten me.

He looked at me as if I was an idiot and stated, "I am the manager on the account and only my name can be on it for fraud reasons."

"What? My salary is being deposited into that checking account and I can't access it?"

"You are the contingency on the account, and you can look at it."

The next day I went to the bank and explained what I had been told by Glen. The banker said that more than one person could be on that account, but my name was not on it, and he couldn't give me any more information. The banker was visibly uncomfortable as I was trying to work this out.

I was able to look at our savings account, as that was a joint account. It had $247 in it.

That evening, I asked Glen, "Where is the $20,000 from my fathers' inheritance? It is no longer in our joint savings account."

He responded, "The money is in a home equity savings account. (Not a thing.) Wikipedia the meaning of home equity savings and then I will show you the account."

He then told me that he had figured out the problem. He explained, "Molly changed her account to just her name, and it messed up all the accounts."

He was upset that Molly, as a twenty-year-old, had deleted his name from her personal account so he could no longer monitor her spending. This lack of control infuriated Glen.

Note how confusing this story is to even follow. It is full of lies and there is only a loose line of connection between the responses he gives and the actual topic.

This is all very typical of a gaslighting incident. This constant changing of the story makes it hard to keep your bearings. The foundation is always shifting.

There are so many aspects to hate about this gaslighting event! What I hate the most, however, is that he was so condescending to me. Giving me an assignment to look up the definition for something before he would grace me with information about our family finances! The audacity! How about, instead, you just tell me how much damn money I have? How about you Wikipedia the definition of giant pain in my ass?

۞

I received additional money from my father's inheritance. I wanted to use this specifically for a basement remodel, as my father had lived in our basement for a while during the building of his house. My father had passed away one year prior, and I wanted the kids to know the basement remodel was from their grandfather.

I put this money in a newly opened checking account in just my name. I had finally learned that money disappeared when Glen had access.

The remodel was an uphill battle, as Glen wanted to use the inheritance for something else. I don't know what, as I was not privy to that kind of information. He constantly badgered me to move it over to our joint savings. No thank you!

I worked with a designer and had the full remodel within the budget. I had discussed this at length with Glen and had shown him the plans. I got a quote for a television with surround sound, but it was ridiculously expensive, so I scaled it down to the speakers for the time being. We already had a sufficient TV and we could upgrade later.

I then had the designer help me figure out where to place the furniture and the speakers. This was all marked on the ceiling, and I had discussed this with the electrician and Glen. I was not home when the workers arrived, so Glen unilaterally decided to move the speaker locations. Annoying, but whatever! I decided that was not worth a fight.

Glen still insisted upon a new, huge TV. We discussed this and I explained my reasoning for waiting. I wanted to stay in budget from the inheritance and I was concerned about the slim joint savings account.

Whenever Glen wanted something, he bought it. He would say, "We discussed this." Technically, we had discussed it but had not agreed. So, he did what he wanted.

I was at work and Hunter, age twelve, called to tell me that Glen was on his way to buy the TV. This made Hunter nervous, because he had overheard the prior discussions.

I called Glen and he was, indeed, on his way to get the TV.

I told him, "I am uncomfortable spending money that we don't have."

He said, "You put it on a credit card and pay it back thirty days later."

"It is not that I don't understand how credit cards work. I definitely don't want to buy a new TV."

Again, note the gaslighting change in the topic of concern. There is always a thread of truth or connection. The topic was about financial concerns and that became about him lecturing me on how a credit card works. He was attempting to keep me off balance.

Additionally, he was throwing in the added abuse of implying I was stupid for not knowing how a credit card works.

As if it was the point of no return, he added, "I am already in the car." He bought the TV.

When I arrived home from work, he was in the process of mounting it on the wall with his brother. I asked for the receipt, and he said it was in his office. His home office was a disaster that was basically a pile of disorganized papers. Oddly, the multiple drawers were basically empty. I looked on the top layer for a receipt. Surprise, not anywhere to be found!

I changed into my running clothes, took off down the road, called my brother, Mark, and we talked through my plan for escape.

I knew I had to leave but I was so worried about how this would affect the kids, whose ages ranged from twelve to twenty years old.

I said, "I just can't do it. I can't do this to my kids."

Mark answered with the wisest words, "You are not doing this to your kids, Glen is. You are saving yourself and your kids. Glen is going to bankrupt you. I am coming to your house on Monday, and I will be there when you give him the divorce papers."

Mark lived four hours away and took a day off work to be by my side. He totally had my back.

When I said something to Glen later that evening about the TV, he said, "It was your decision to buy the TV."

Oh right, everything is my fault, I forgot.

He rationalized this by stating the cost of the TV he had bought was less than the TV that was in the bid. Since I had gotten the bid, I was the one that wanted the TV. One plus one equals . . . whatever the hell Glen says it equals.

In the entirety of our twenty-four-year marriage, we never, ever, sat down and went through our finances.

Chapter 33

Divorce Filed

A few days before filing for divorce, I was riding with Maria to the state cross country meet to watch our children compete. We were visiting and she told me the story of her grandmother. Her grandmother was involved in a decades-long, bad relationship with her alcoholic husband, whom she never left.

At the end of the story, Maria added, "My grandmother had a really bad life."

My heart caught in my throat, and it started to race.

Oh no! I thought. *My life is bad. My life story is bad!*

I knew at that point that I would spend my next several months, years, whatever, to rewrite my story. I did not want my children or grandchildren to ever describe me that way. It is just so tragic to waste a life!

So, I filed for divorce in October 2014, after twenty-four years of marriage. I had stood on the edge of the cliff for years and then I finally jumped. I could never go back to life before the jump. There was no tether. The words were said, and the papers were filed. There was a clarity just before the jump that was not present prior to that time. I had no other choice. I knew the water at the end of my fall would be warm, fulfilling, and soul-healing. I did not know, however, how long the fall would last or how many times I would bang against the side of the cliff during the fall.

The issues, described in the prior chapters, served as the battleground for the war I endured for decades. The only way to survive was to exit the war. It was not a war I was going to win. The marriage was not salvageable. I had fallen out of love. For the last several years of our marriage, I had a hard time telling Glen that I loved him. He would tell me he loved me until the bitter end, but that wasn't love. It was a game of his, a manipulation, to get me to say it back. Narcissists aren't capable of deep, compassionate love. He never genuinely loved me, so the end of our love was not different for him.

Because of a bizarre and dangerous South Dakota law, neither party in a divorce is allowed to move out of the marital home until both parties agree and a document is signed. Technically, you are not a prisoner and can leave, but in the eyes of the law, leaving is considered abandonment of the house and the kids. And then, good luck trying to get possession of the house or custody of the kids in divorce court.

Think for a moment how perilous that situation has the potential to be. In my particular situation, I filed for divorce from a narcissist. Divorce constitutes a major "narcissistic injury." In psychological terms, a "narcissistic injury" is a wound to their ego so severe that it can trigger intense emotional reactions, including anger, denial, or retaliatory behavior.

As I've said, narcissists often rely on external validation—especially from romantic partners—to support their fragile self-esteem and inflated self-image. When a partner leaves through divorce, it:

- Shatters their control: Narcissists need to feel in control of the relationship. Divorce is a rejection they can't manipulate.

- Threatens their ego: The separation signals that they are no longer "wanted" or "admired," which is intolerable to them.

- Publicly exposes failure: Divorce can feel like humiliation or failure in front of others, damaging their carefully crafted image.

- Triggers rage or revenge: The perceived abandonment or betrayal may provoke narcissistic rage, blame-shifting, or attempts to punish the ex.

So, now I am expected to just live with this unstable person after inflicting that injury? It is unfathomable to me that anyone would think that is a good, or safe, plan.

Glen outweighed me by 120 pounds and had an arsenal of guns. Also, given his possession of a Y chromosome, he had more testosterone and therefore more muscle mass.

Was I certain Glen would hurt me? No. Was I certain he would not? Also, no.

Glen refused to leave, so it was up to me to leave the marital home. He kept telling me to leave, but he would not sign the damn form. I was trapped in my own home.

One morning as I was leaving for work, Glen came into the garage as I was pulling out.

He motioned for me to open the window and when I did, he asked, "Did you find an apartment? Your time is running out."

My time is running out. My time is running out. I. Was. Forced. To. Live. With. This. Man!

One morning, at 3:55 a.m., I awoke to Glen speaking loudly and aggressively in the bedroom where I was sleeping.

"Where are the credit card statements?" he demanded. "They are not in my office!"

I awoke with a start. My heart was pounding, and I was trying to comprehend what he was saying. I responded, "I don't know."

"Have you removed any valuables from the house?"

"What? Let's talk about this during the day."

"Where is your pistol?" he asked.

I had inherited a fifty-magnum pistol from my uncle about a year earlier. I wasn't sure what I should do with it as I have never had an interest in guns, let alone one that size. But I still had it.

"It is in the closet where you put it. I haven't moved it."

He retrieved the gun and left the room.

I was awake for the rest of the night, which was likely his goal.

I would love for any judge to look me in the eye and tell me that living with this man was a safe plan.

*

Another day, Glen called me while I was working at the hospital and said, "A priest from the diocese called and needs to talk to you. The priest found out that you filed, probably from your lawyer. This is a legal matter and since we are Catholic, this needs to be discussed with the priest. I am going to give the priest your cell number. This is the kind of stuff you are going to have to do now." A priest never called me.

❦

About six months prior to starting the divorce process, Glen started sleeping in the bedroom in the basement. There was no specific fight or discussion of this. He just started doing it. So, after I filed for divorce, I kept sleeping in the master bedroom and he continued sleeping downstairs.

After about two months, Glen came into the master bedroom one morning and announced, "We will be switching rooms every week, so you need to move downstairs, and I am taking the master bedroom." He added, "You filed, so it is going to be inconvenient for you." This was a Saturday morning, just as I was leaving to start my weekend on call. I came home at the end of a long day, to find Glen spread out, starfish style, across the bed in the master bedroom. He was grinning in a way that I will remember forever. It was a smug and dickish grin letting me know that he had control over me and all our possessions.

I grabbed the suitcases and started loading them up. I hauled all my stuff down the two floors, cleaned up the basement, and rearranged it to my liking.

While I did this, Glen kept saying that I didn't need to move downstairs, and we could just share the room.

He said, "I know you don't like this."

I coolly responded, "I don't mind this. I will never share a bedroom with you ever again."

So now I was living in the basement of the house that I had paid for, while Glen claimed the rest of the house as his domain. I cleaned it all up and arranged it how I liked. When I would leave the house, or sometimes while I slept, Glen would rearrange the basement furniture. He would move the couch so close to the huge TV that you couldn't see it well, like sitting too close to the screen at the theater. He would also move the exercise equipment. He was basically moving it back to the way it was before I began living down there.

He was letting me know the house was his.

The rearranging of the furniture felt like a metaphor for my life. I would think there was some semblance of organization to my life when I went to bed, but I would wake up in a rearranged world. I would eventually find my way back out, but there were periods of disorientation and lots of bruises along the way.

Around this same time frame, I was out of town for a meeting with a world-renowned neurologist to discuss my headache research. Glen knew this was an important meeting. While I was speaking with this neurologist, Glen called and texted me multiple times. I excused myself and stepped out of the room, as I was worried there was an emergency with the kids. Glen asked me where Sawyer and the pickup were. He said he was concerned that Sawyer had run away because of the divorce.

I called Sawyer, as I knew he was the reliable source about what was occurring.

To my relief, Sawyer answered right away. After I explained what Glen had told me, Sawyer responded in disgust, "Dad knows where I am. He sent me to town with the pickup to get a tractor part."

Sawyer also told me he was frustrated because he got to the tractor supply store only to find out that Glen already had someone else pick up the part.

Sawyer added that he was driving from the store to Maria and Jacob's house to do some work they had asked him to do. He said he was almost there, and that Glen knew this plan.

As I was still on the phone, Sawyer said, "That is weird. Dad is following me in his vehicle."

Glen followed Sawyer into our friend's driveway and got out of his car to stand by Sawyer. Maria came outside and witnessed Glen yelling at Sawyer. She later told me it was very upsetting as she couldn't even tell what Glen was yelling at Sawyer about. She said Glen was totally irrational.

After Glen left, she asked Sawyer if he was okay and offered the option of him staying at their house until I returned. He declined with a shrug, stating, "Dad acts like that all the time, so I am used to it."

✻

I needed a sanity break, so Molly and I traveled to Maine to visit Laura, my best friend from my residency years.

While we were there, the chaos continued at home.

Sawyer had finished his Eagle Scout project, in which he made a sign for the Senior Citizen Center. Glen was helping Sawyer get this sign to the center. Meanwhile, I received several calls from Glen in a fully irrational mode. He was shouting at me, intermixed with yelling at Sawyer. He wanted me to tell Sawyer to do what he said. Despite trying, I could not tell what Glen wanted me to tell Sawyer.

Glen yelled so often that it had become his form of talking at home. The kids became desensitized to this. The problem occurred when the yelled commands became varied, and they couldn't understand what he wanted.

But this time it was too much, and Sawyer was upset. He just wanted Glen to leave him alone so he could do the project himself.

I told Glen to stop yelling, as it was upsetting Sawyer and I didn't want him distracted when he left there to drive the sign to town.

Charles was witnessing this play out. He decided to drive Sawyer and help him get the sign put up. On the drive, a deer ran in front of Charles, and he had the full presence of mind to avoid hitting the deer. I worried Sawyer may not have been able to do that if he was driving while upset.

The level of distress you get from gaslighting is not the same as other forms of being yelled at or scolded. It comes with an additional level of frustration because you have so much trouble keeping up with the changing platform of demands, etc.

Molly and I drove to Kansas City for a wedding shower for a niece on Glen's side of the family. I had almost completed the six-hour drive when Glen started repetitively calling me because he was mad at Charles. I don't even remember what he was mad about. I was so concerned about Charles' emotional safety that I turned the car around and started heading back home to protect him. Somehow the situation calmed down enough for me to stay in Kansas. I don't know if this was because I had told him I was going to head home or what happened. By this point, I was realizing that Glen tended to escalate in his abuse of the kids when I was out of town.

So, life continued and of course another event was soon to follow.

Glen left to pick Hunter up from basketball practice.

It was evening and Glen called me right after he left the house. He said, "There is someone driving around in our slough. If it isn't Sawyer, you better call the cops."

I looked out the window and didn't see any vehicle lights in the dark night. Sawyer came into the house. I asked him about this, and he said he was not driving in the slough, but that dad called him and said, "There is some weird stuff going on lately and mom has been calling the cops."

Glen's ability to confabulate stories was impressive! Too bad he didn't put this skill to use with something more productive than agitating me and the kids.

Glen had a very chaotic sleep schedule, as is common with people with NPD. After I had moved into the basement, I awoke at 3:15 a.m. with him standing beside my bed, leaning over me.

Alarmed and unnerved that he was in the room, and hovering over me, I asked, "What are you doing?"

"I am looking to see if Hunter is in your bed."

Hunter's bedroom was upstairs, on the level where Glen was sleeping.

I mused, "Is Hunter missing or is Glen messing with me?"

I am sure from what you have read so far that you all know that answer.

After Glen left my room, I listened to hear if he was walking around anymore. When his footsteps stopped, and the house was silent, I tiptoed to Hunter's room and found him sound asleep.

Yes, I tiptoed. I was scared, in my own home and of my own husband.

✿

By Christmas time, I was two months into the divorce process and still living in the marital home. Glen came down to the basement to inform me that my family was not allowed to come to our house for our annual Christmas celebration. We had been hosting this for eighteen years by this time, so clearly it was our family tradition. We had to pivot and celebrate at a hotel instead.

Molly asked me why the party could not be at our house. She said, "Dad said the Christmas party can't be at our house because the lawyers won't allow it." She was aware it was Glen who wouldn't allow it, so she asked me why Glen would say something like that.

It was difficult to explain to her why her father was lying. There was no viable explanation.

While he was in town for the Christmas celebration, my brother, Mark, came to the house to get stuff from my dad's estate, including two snow blowers. Mark asked to borrow my inherited gun, as he wanted to use this for an Alaskan hunting trip. I couldn't access the gun because Glen had placed it in the gun safe. Of course, I was not allowed to have that combination.

When Mark and I were driving away from the house, Glen passed us in his vehicle going the other way. Glen called me to see what we were doing at the house, reminding me that my family was not allowed there. I told him my brother had taken my father's two snow blowers. I also told him I needed to get my gun for Mark to borrow.

Mark and I went back to the house. When we got there, Glen had already removed the gun from the safe and he had it in the kitchen.

Glen asked me, "Do you have the paperwork for this gun stating that it is yours?"

I said, "You and I both know that gun is mine."

Glen rolled his eyes at me and then told Mark he could take the gun for the hunt, but he needed to give it back after that, as it was part of the marital property. He handed the gun to Mark.

That gun was an inherited gift to me and Glen had no legal right to it.

While at the house, Mark helped me change my bedroom and bathroom doors to keyed locks.

When Glen noticed the doorknobs were changed, he said, "You do not have permission to alter the house. I am going to take off the locks."

Glen then called all four kids into the living room and said, "Mom is acting weird. She put locks on the doors. She is probably scared for her life."

When I walked past him later in the evening, he chanted repeatedly, "Paranoia will destroy you." When Mark and I changed the bedroom lock, we noticed one of the pins was not flush in the hinge. Mark tried to get it flush, but was not successful, as it just wouldn't move.

The next weekend, I came home from being out of town for two days. I was unlocking my bedroom door and stopped short. My stomach flipped. The pin in the hinge was now flush. I knew instantly that Glen had removed the door and had been in my room.

A few days later, Glen repeated something that I had privately told my mother while we were in my bedroom. I can't recall exactly what he quoted, but I do remember that it was something inconsequential and it didn't involve him.

I am certain a recording device had been placed in my room.

The first Christmas Day was rough. We opened gifts together on Christmas morning, but then Glen took the kids to his family's celebration. I was home alone all afternoon. I cleaned up the house from the morning gift opening and went for a run in an attempt to distract myself. This was the only time, ever, that I contemplated just staying in the marriage to avoid being away from my kids. Fortunately, Maria was willing to talk this through with me, putting me back on track and confirming my resolve.

As an additional distraction, I had planned on going to a movie that was opening on Christmas Day. This was the movie version of a beloved book, and I was eagerly anticipating its release. Molly and Charles got home in the late afternoon, and they said they wanted to go with me. They were eighteen and twenty years old at that time. Sawyer, who was sixteen, rode home with Charles and Molly after asking Glen if it was okay for him to leave the party. Sawyer stayed home alone while we went to the movie, as he did not want to go. Glen then claimed, to his lawyer, that I had Sawyer for the entire Christmas evening and because of that he would be able to have them for Christmas Day the next year as well.

During this time, Molly was still on college break and Glen wanted her to move her car so he could scoop snow. She told him she would do it in a few minutes. She was working on a knitting project and wanted to finish the row, which she explained to him.

He quickly became agitated and yelled, "Ever since your mom filed for divorce, you guys think you can act like this."

When she went out to move her car a couple minutes later, Glen told her, "I am going to invite Grandma Kay (his mother) over because you need a more positive female influence in your life."

Molly said, "If Grandma Kay comes over, I am going to have her talk to her son."

Good gut punch, Molly!

❀

On a snowy and icy evening over Christmas break from college, Charles left for a babysitting job in his little Jetta, my old one. On his drive, he slid, and the front wheels of his front wheel drive became stuck in the snow and ice on the edge of the gravel road. Sawyer, who was sixteen, gathered up the gear and got into the family Suburban to go help his brother. Glen had been gone, but pulled into the driveway as Sawyer was backing out of the garage.

Glen asked Sawyer where he was going.

Sawyer said he was going to help Charles. He told him that Charles was stuck, and they could do it with just the two of them. Sawyer knew Charles was in a hurry to get to his job.

Sawyer left and Glen came into the house yelling, "I am going to call the sheriff and report the Suburban stolen and then Sawyer can spend the night in juvie (juvenile detention center)." He frequently threatened to take the kids to the juvenile detention center if they didn't do exactly as he said.

"You are crazy in the head!" he yelled. "All this is your fault because you started this, and you are the only one that wants this."

He was referring to the divorce, but yelling this out of context, and in front of Hunter.

I drove to the spot where Charles was stuck so he could take my car to the babysitting job. Sawyer and I worked on getting the car out of the ditch. By this time, it was still snowing and was really blowing.

Then Glen drove up to the stuck car and started yelling

unintelligibly at us as he started to get the car hooked up to pull it out. Sawyer was doing his best to ignore the yelling and working on the task at hand. This was difficult in the frigid weather with the snow blowing.

The situation was totally out of control by this point, so I called Glen's brother to help with the car. This particular brother was adept at calming Glen down. Once he arrived, I took Sawyer and drove home. It was always best to leave any situation where Glen was out of control. Staying would only prolong the abuse, and the situation would not improve.

❦

On another snowy evening about one month later, I was sitting in my basement bedroom watching the news. A blizzard was predicted to occur through the night and into the next day. I knew we would all need four-wheel drive vehicles to get to school and work in the morning. We had three appropriate winter vehicles, one for Glen, one for me, and one for the boys. This would work out great, except working out great never happened in our house.

I told Glen, "There is going to be a blizzard, so I need to take the Suburban to work tomorrow. You can take the GMC truck, and the boys can take the Chevy pickup."

I would have typically driven my Jetta, but that was too light, and it was not a four-wheel drive.

Glen turned from me and immediately went out to the garage, locked the Suburban and GMC and took the keys.

He said, "You can drive the Chevy." He then added, "I made the plan."

The old Chevy pickup was what the boys usually drove. And it was out of gas.

I got bundled up in my winter gear to head to the gas station and went back to the kitchen to ask Glen for the Chevy keys. Glen wasn't there, so I went upstairs. I stood in the hall just outside the master bedroom, which was slightly ajar, and asked him for the keys.

Glen hollered, "Rape! Rape! Rape!"

Woah! What the hell? I was flabbergasted and briefly immobilized by this bizarre and outlandish accusation.

Recall that part of gaslighting is a rocking of your foundation. I had somehow slid from making a plan for the next day into a dystopian world in which I was being accused of raping someone who was in a different room.

He made this insane claim with the kids well within hearing range.

To break this cycle, I simply walked back downstairs without responding. I was feeling so defeated. *What had my life become?*

Sawyer came down and said, "I am going to fill the Chevy with gas so I can drive it tomorrow."

It was 10 p.m. by that time, so I told him not to do that. I said I would just drive the Chevy to make things easiest for everyone and I would leave early enough to get gas in the morning.

Sawyer looked sad and walked back up to his bedroom.

We were all just so defeated with our situation, and we had no idea how long that phase of being forced to live under one roof would last. Again, thank you to the legal system for making this happen. *So frikken dumb and dangerous!*

When I awoke the next morning, Glen had already left the house, with the GMC. He left the Suburban for me and the Chevy for the boys. The key was in the Suburban. So, exactly as I had suggested the night prior.

This was simply a game for him.

When I woke Hunter for school, the first thing he anxiously said was, "What vehicle are you driving?"

"It is all worked out and I have a safe vehicle."

Later that morning, I got a call from my friend, Maria, telling me that Glen had sent out a group text at 10:30 p.m. the prior evening.

She sent me the text that went exactly like this, *"Carol will have a ATV (he means four-wheel drive) tomorrow she needs to relax thanks for your support Sorry for the unusual text last night Carol was very upset she told Huntor (he regularly spelled Hunter's name wrong) that I was not giving her a four-wheel-drive vehicle and that she would probably die in a car accident she did have a four-wheel-drive car to drive today of course I let her have the suburban for the day Huntor said that she had text everybody in this group text last night asking for a ride"*

Of course, this made no sense to her as I had sent no such text and had not called anyone.

This should have been such an easy issue. Switch the Jetta for the Suburban. Done in a few seconds. But that is not life with a narcissist. This is gaslighting.

Also, note the subtlety of his email in which he states, "I let her have the suburban." It was a family vehicle, but he considered everything to be his property, yet I alone had paid for that vehicle before Glen even had a job.

✿

I woke up at 6:30 a.m. on a Saturday for a full weekend of being on call. I got ready and headed upstairs to leave.

Glen was sitting at the table and said, "I am having a party tonight and you are invited if you want to come." I replied warily, "We can't have a party tonight. I am on call." He said, "You agreed to move out of here this week, so that is too bad." I reminded him, "You have not signed the stipulation that allows me to leave!"

"I sent a document stating what you could take from the house."

I retorted, "That has nothing to do with the stipulation stating I can move out. You can't trap me here and then tell me to leave."

He didn't have any people over, and instead he attended a previously scheduled couples shower for his niece.

✿

My brother, Mark, informed me that he had received an email from Glen. This had been sent to all my siblings, their spouses, and several of my friends.

This email stated, *"Everything Carol is saying about me is 100% inaccurate Carol wants the divorce because she needs a change. I don't know what is wrong with her but she changed after her dad died."*

He had a total lack of insight into the issues that had led to the filing, except the part about me needing a change. That part was true! I needed out of the marriage; I needed to be away from my abuser.

In addition, yet again, he was implying that I am emotionally unstable. This time because of my father's death. This was Glen's distortion campaign to try to get others to question my sanity and my decision. He was attempting to regain some power and control.

⚜

My mother was staying with me for five weeks, in part to support me, but also because she was having heart issues. Her cardiologist saw patients in the hospital where I worked, and mom lived about five hours away. Actually, during part of this five-week period, she was admitted to the hospital.

Glen texted me, "*$485 our house utilities went up with your mom living there the last five weeks / $100 a week for rental is fair please issue me a check.*"

I responded, "*She is not paying rent to visit me.*"

"*I will add the bill to your ledger.*"

A ledger! He always told me that he had a ledger to keep track of everything that I owed him.

⚜

Glen got home from work about 7:30 p.m. and went right up to his room. Hunter, Sawyer, and I had already eaten supper and were in my basement bedroom. I was reading and the boys were playing video games. At 10 p.m., Glen called me on my cell phone and told me to have the boys come upstairs. Hunter had fallen asleep, so I told Glen he was going to sleep in my room, which had a king size bed and two twin beds all set up. Glen came down and hollered through my closed door for Hunter to go upstairs. This woke Hunter up, so he went upstairs.

Upstairs, Glen started yelling at the boys. I couldn't tell what he was even yelling about, but he was getting everyone wound up and it was 10:20 p.m. I told the boys to just come back downstairs so they could sleep. Sawyer said he was just going to his room, but Hunter came downstairs with me.

Glen then called 911, stating that I was keeping the kids from him.

He said, "She has Hunter on lock down" and "she kidnapped him."

The deputy came to the house at 10:40 p.m. This obviously kept the kids up and scared Hunter. The deputies interviewed Glen, me, and Sawyer independently. The deputy told me, "It is not kidnapping if you are in the same home."

I said, "I know. I didn't call you."

I find it odd that he assumed that I was the one who had made this ridiculous accusation.

My poor kids, living in this totally dysfunctional situation. Again, thank you very much to the legal system!

A couple weeks later, I picked Hunter up after school. He didn't feel well, so I brought him home and gave him ibuprofen and ginger ale. I then made supper while he rested. After supper, he sat on my bed and did his homework. He fell asleep on my bed while petting his dog.

Glen got home at 9:45 p.m. He came downstairs and

hollered at Hunter from my doorway several times, awakening Hunter.

Glen said, "Hunter better be upstairs in the next five minutes, or I am calling the cops."

Hunter heard this and got up to walk upstairs.

Glen said, "You are withholding the kids from me and that is a form of child abuse."

✶

Glen emailed me:

"You removed documents from my bedroom this weekend. Those items where requested by you and your Lawyer. Your removal of these documents will continue to slow down the process of completion of the interrogatories. You need to stop this behavior."

Of course, I had not been in his room to remove documents, but rather this was his excuse for not having his interrogatories done. By this point, he was already six months past the deadline. Glen then sent an additional email, stating: *"I checked my micro camera and caught you removing those documents."*

That imaginary video never surfaced.

Glen did eventually complete the interrogatories. Several of his answers were, "See wife's answers to interrogatories."

Just like our entire marriage, I was carrying the team.

Chapter 34

Witnessing a Gaslighting Episode

My brother, Mark, came to town to gather some items from our father's storage unit. My father had died about eighteen months earlier, and Mark was executor of the estate.

The key for Dad's storage unit was missing from the key organizer in our kitchen, where all our family keys hung.

I texted Glen, *"I need the key to my dad's storage unit."*

He texted back, *"I will be right home."*

Mark and I loaded some of dad's stuff from the house into Mark's vehicle.

Glen came home and told us, "Nothing of value can be removed from the house."

I flatly stated, "This is stuff that was my dad's. You can look at what we put in the car."

He declined to look, but added, "I called the deputy sheriff, and he will be out to the house in about twenty minutes."

We asked Glen for the storage key again. He said he looked but couldn't find it. Glen left our house and texted Mark, *"meet me at the storage unit alone."*

He added, *"I have taken a full inventory of Earl's stuff and I can tell you everything that is in there."*

This was news to Mark and me, as Glen had no reason to do this and had no business being in the unit.

Mark and I, together, went to the storage unit and Glen was there. Fortunately, Mark had added an additional lock on the unit the day I filed for the divorce, so Glen was unable to open it. While we were at the unit, Glen again said he couldn't find the key, but a few minutes later produced a key from the vehicle he was driving. This was the keychain that the storage lock key had been on, but it didn't unlock the lock.

He said that he had gotten this key from his father, who "had the spare." Keep in mind, this was my family's storage unit, yet Glen and his father had keys?! Well, not really, as he was lying about his father having the keychain in Glen's possession. That was definitely the same keychain that had been on our key rack at home.

Mark and I returned home and found Glen foraging around the house. He said he had some keys to try and left for about fifteen minutes while Mark and I ate supper. The storage unit was about six miles from our home.

Upon Glen's return, Mark asked Glen, "Did you try the keys?"

Glen said, "No, but I have a friend that is a locksmith, and he is going to try to get the lock off now."

I asked him who the locksmith was, and he wouldn't tell me. He did say, "He is a great guy, a real great guy."

Mark and I went back to the storage unit, and the old lock had been removed. We opened the unit and found that it had been fully rearranged from the last time either of us had been there.

Glen had unlocked this himself. There was no locksmith involved.

Mark said, "You know when he referred to the locksmith as a great guy, he was referring to himself, right?"

This was the first gaslighting incident Mark had been involved in. He was surprised that this was what I had been living with.

The sheriff never came.

Chapter 35

I Finally Move Out

Six months after I filed for divorce, I was "allowed" to move out of the marital home. By this time, my world had grown very small. I was only allowed in the basement, other than passing through the kitchen on my way to the basement or back to the garage. Glen had continued to rearrange the furniture in the basement living room area. I had given up on that fruitless and frustrating battle, left it as it was, and just stayed out of that area. I only occupied my bedroom and bathroom.

Whenever I left my two rooms, I faced verbal attacks, until the fear and exhaustion became too much—and I barely left at all. This was all Glen's attempt to maintain control over me, as I am sure on some level he knew he was losing control. I was gaining control of myself.

✿

I was physically and psychologically fading away. My appetite was gone. When I tried to eat, it was hard to swallow. It always felt like I was on the verge of crying, so I just couldn't swallow past the lump in my throat.

I was losing all hope. The judicial system wasn't helping and was actually placing me in harm's way. I was miserable!

I decided to make this move an adventure for us, the boys and me, so I signed a lease for a downtown loft. This would be a big change, since the boys has grown up in the country. Additionally, they had never lived in an apartment, and I had not lived in one for many years. It felt like I was moving backwards in my life plan, from a house to an apartment, yet the idea of coming home to a downtown loft seemed exciting. I could walk amongst the shops, restaurants, and nightlife to dampen my loneliness when the boys were not with me.

The fact that Glen lived in the marital home, with a pool and thirty-two acres of land, compounded my feeling of unrest. *How had I gotten to this position?* The answer was that I had made a poor choice in a mate.

I just kept reminding myself that everything I was doing now was taking me one step closer to a happier life. But it was a hard, long road. I had to keep in mind that the divorce process was just a small part of my life. I would grind through it and make it to the other side.

When it was time to physically move out of the house, Maria volunteered to help. We did this on a weekday, so Glen would be at work and out of our way. Glen somehow came home in the late morning. How he ever kept a job was beyond my comprehension.

Glen started following us around and taking stuff out of the boxes as fast as we could put them in. I was following the list the lawyers had made us agree upon, yet Glen was not happy with this. Glen always had a hard time getting rid of or losing possession of anything.

He unpacked a couple pictures that he said were his. They were the pictures that Shon's parents had given Shon and me for our wedding, but Glen stated they were a gift from his parents.

I said, "Turn the picture over and you will see the authentication paperwork noting the year of 1986, the year I was married."

Maria said, "Just leave her alone."

Glen put down the pictures, left the room, and called Maria's husband, Jacob.

Glen told him, "Come control your wife."

Jacob came over right away, as he was concerned for our safety. He helped us pack up the rest of my stuff. He then helped us load everything into a trailer and move it to my former mother-in-law's garage. My former brother-in-law came and helped as well. They were all shocked and worried by Glen's behavior. They could see that he was not mentally stable.

Jacob commented, "How is Glen upset about what you are taking? This is a small fraction of what is in that house, shed and barn."

✿

The date of the move was a few days later. While I was getting the rest of the stuff on my list, Sawyer helped me carry a mattress out to the trailer.

Glen saw us and said I could not have that particular mattress. He took the end of the mattress that Sawyer was holding, with me holding onto the other end at the threshold of the front door. He pulled the mattress back into the house. When I didn't let go, he shoved the mattress back toward me, slamming my head into the door frame.

I dropped the mattress and walked toward him until we were just an inch apart. I stared straight into his eyes and his rotten soul. I am not sure why I did this, but I assume it was my limbic "fight" response. His fists flexed and relaxed multiple times at his sides as he held his ground.

I went outside to call Maria to come over. She told me to call the police, which I did.

The police came into the house and told Glen and me to go into the garage. The officer asked me what was going on. When I started to explain what had happened with the mattress, Glen interrupted and yelled that I was lying.

I stopped briefly, but then continued to answer the officer's question.

The cop said, "Both of you stop talking or I will take you both in."

I was dumbfounded. Why was I being told to stop talking when Glen was the one yelling and I was simply answering the question?

The answer is: I was being bundled into the same category as Glen. He was unhinged, so we were both considered unhinged. It was embarrassing to understand at that point that being associated with Glen made me appear just as crazy as him.

I recall a feeling of my heart dropping as I felt so helpless to stick up for myself and my children. I was ultimately on my own.

Thank God that Maria had arrived, or I may have just crumpled onto the floor in despair. She kept me focused on the goal of getting out of the house that night.

❦

My loft was not ready when I left for a work trip to California for a few days. So, I had moved out of my house and was not yet in the loft. All my stuff was at my former mother-in-law's house and in a storage unit. Upon my return from California, I walked to my car in the airport parking lot. My piece-of-shit, 2009 VW, manual, Jetta was my only private space. I was literally homeless. And, I would not have the boys for two more days. Homeless and no kids!

With each step, I was coming closer to the brink of crying. I barely made it to my car before the weight of all that hit me, and I started crying hysterically. The kind of crying that makes you short of breath and leaves you with spasms of your diaphragm.

I drove to the river and tried to find some peace, as water is my calming medium. I called my sister, Amelia, and then Jenny, my neurologist friend. They both worked to calm me, but I was almost inconsolable.

How was I at this point in life? Had I not done all the right things? I had a good job, yet I was homeless because of the person I married. Everything was crashing down on me. I didn't know how I would survive. I didn't know how to survive.

I pulled myself together eventually and drove to Sawyer's track meet. When Hunter saw my car pull into the parking lot, he came running toward me and gave me a hug. That saved me! I was going to make it!

❀

As the divorce was progressing slowly, we started the child custody arrangement. The transitions from one parent to the other were uncomfortable because I would need to briefly interact with Glen. With each transition, Glen seemed to escalate in his inability to control his dissatisfaction with the whole process.

By the third child exchange, Glen started his gaslighting. The agreed upon transition time was 5 p.m. It was the end of my time, so I was at the school to pick Hunter up at 3:30 p.m. As I waited in my car, I saw Glen pull into the parking lot and then walk into the school. What was he up to?

I quickly checked my email, as that was our mode of communication. There was an email from Glen. He said: *"Last Friday you had Molly pick up Hunter at 3:30 from school and he was at your place by 4:10 pm. I did not see him again until today. To correct your violation of Parenting law, I will pick up Hunter at 3:30 today to correct your wrongdoing."*

Molly had been in town the weekend prior and had asked Glen if she could pick him up from the school. He had agreed. I had not been any part of that exchange.

Had he emailed me sooner, I would have just let this happen, but I had no idea that he had planned to pick up Hunter. I could have stayed at work rather than rushing around.

I followed Glen into the school and walked up to him. I quietly reminded him that I had Hunter until 5 p.m.

He said, "Check your email. I am getting him now because of your wrongdoing."

I asked Hunter's homeroom teacher, who was standing near us, to assist, as I did not want a scene. We walked down the hall with Glen whispering to the teacher while I walked behind them. I then saw Hunter come from a side hallway. I pivoted that direction and told him quietly to just come with me.

Hunter walked with me out the door and got into the car. Glen came to the car to talk to Hunter, reached into my car, and took the garage door opener to the marital home that was hanging on my visor. He didn't ask for it, he just violated my space without even asking me to give it to him.

I told him that Hunter needed to get his things, but we would be at the transition spot by 5 p.m.

Hunter and I went to the loft to gather his things and then drove to Subway by 4:45 p.m. I texted Glen to let him know that we were at the front of the building.

Glen called at 4:50 p.m. stating, "I will meet you at the loft because the dog is supposed to come with Hunter."

I tried to explain that the dog, Goldie, would go with Sawyer in one hour, as Hunter didn't want Goldie to ride in Glen's new car. Hunter said he had already explained this to Glen on the phone as well.

I texted Glen, *"We are waiting for you at Subway. I am not going to the loft right now."*

Glen called Hunter again and told him to come to the back side of Subway and to "bring Charles' trumpet."

Of course, we didn't randomly have the trumpet with us, but this was gaslighting.

Eventually Glen met us and by this point Hunter was very frustrated. It broke my heart to see Hunter leave with his unstable father.

❦

Molly was in town and texted Glen that she was on her way to the marital home. He called her and said, "You need to answer some questions before you drive here."

Molly said, "So I am not able to come to my own house?"

Glen replied, "You can't if you are unable to answer some questions. You can't come here if you are going to spy on me. I need people around me that care about me. Your mom is the one that wanted the divorce and now I am finding out the reasons why."

He asked her several questions, including, "Did you give mom the code to the lock box on the garage door? Did you know that mom has been in the house in the last couple days?"

Since I value my life and since my children can only depend on me, I most certainly would not enter a house with a crazy person who owns twenty-seven guns and hates me. For cripes' sakes, as my grandma would say.

Glen also added, "I do not want you out here if you are going to take pictures of my house. You shouldn't have told mom that I bought a car. I know she sat you down and inter- rogated you about it. My lawyer and I had it all planned out and now I am in trouble, and it cost me $1,000 in lawyer fees to straighten it out."

Glen had bought this car against a restraining order in which we were not to make any major purchases during the divorce process. Glen already had a pickup and Suburban. The kids of driving age each had their own vehicle as well.

Glen was obsessed with keeping everything, so he needed to buy a new car to replace the one I took, my own vehicle.

As he was nearing the end of his interrogation of our daughter, he asked, "Was mom driving when the Chevy was damaged?"

Molly told Glen, again, that her boyfriend had been driving when he hit something and got a small dent. I was not even in the vehicle or surrounding area.

Molly ended up calling Charles to talk this through with him, as my two oldest children were the most fluent in "Glen talk." I heard Charles on the phone telling her not to drive until she could calm down, as she was crying so hard after the interrogation and feeling unwelcome in her home where her siblings were staying.

I told him to tell her to just come to the loft and not engage with Glen's behavior further. Molly then called Hunter and Sawyer individually to tell them that she was not coming to see them at the house, and she would see them when they came to the loft in two days.

Molly told me she felt so bad choosing her mental health and standing her ground with Glen over "just sucking it up" and enduring the verbal attack to spend time with her younger siblings.

It is just terrible that her own father would do this to her. But, narcissists only love themselves.

Glen would not allow me to even drive onto the driveway to drop off the kids. I was told to drop the kids off at the church across the highway. The boys then had to walk across the highway and down the 200-yard driveway, no matter the weather conditions or time of day or night. He even made Hunter do this when he was on crutches.

I once received a text from Glen after I had dropped Hunter and Goldie off at the church, stating, *"Do not make Goldie & Hunter cross the highway any mor that is 2 dagerous think"*

I responded, *"YOU are the one making him cross the road since YOU won't let me drive down the driveway for the transitions. Plus, I was watching for cars and I told him when to go. Plus he is 14 and drives so I think he knows when it is safe to cross. Stop harassing me."*

Glen responded with two messages:

"I think you can figure out that it's not safe to drop a kid off and have them cross a highway with his dog without a leash on" and *"I want you to tell me why you cannot come on the property"*

I did not respond after that. His texts were just too ludicrous.

On another transition day, I texted Glen at 4:15 p.m.: *"Meet me at Subway. I will be there at 5 p.m."*

He answered, *"Drop Hunter off at my parents and then Sawyer can pick him up after track."*

I found this odd, as this was not a typical transition site. Also, dropping him off at his parents' house added about half an hour to my drive. This required that I leave earlier from work, which I had not planned for. I started rushing to get everything wrapped up at work as I could already tell this was going to turn into a shit show.

Glen called Hunter and told him he would go to his uncle's house instead (Glen's brother). Hunter told Glen he wanted to stay with me until Glen got home.

Hunter asked Glen where he was and Glen said, "I can't talk now."

This was a typical tactic for Glen to get off the phone quickly when he didn't want to disclose information.

I texted Glen, *"I will bring Hunter to Subway at 5 , and you can decide which of your family members picks him up."*

At 5:05 p.m., I was at Subway and Glen texted: *"Drop Hunter off at my brothers."*

I drove to his brother's and the only person home was his sister-in-law, who had no idea Hunter was coming and she had company. I explained that I was not part of the plan, but this was what I had been instructed to do.

It turned out that Glen was five hours away and didn't pick Hunter up until 10 p.m. This was all time that I could have spent with Hunter, rather than dropping him off with someone who was busy and would not even be interacting with him.

Glen's only goal with his parenting time was keeping the kids from me. The goal was not what was best for the boys.

❧

I bought Hunter his first iPhone for his thirteenth birthday. This was the only thing he had asked for and he was elated when he opened his gift. He texted his siblings right away and then spent most of that evening getting his phone set up.

But then it was time for Hunter to go to The House I Paid For. I could call it "The House I Paid For But Am Not Allowed In," but that is really cumbersome.

Glen took Hunter's phone immediately and told him, "I am going to trade it in for a better phone."

Hunter called me from the home phone, devastated and tearful, and said, "Mom, that was my big present."

I usually give my kids one big present and a few small ones for birthdays and Christmas.

I texted Glen, *"Where is my phone?"*

He called me and said, "I turned it into Verizon already. You need to give the box to me so you can be credited."

When I asked him more about this, he hung up on me.

I called Verizon and asked them about this and, predictably, they knew nothing about what I was asking. *Ughhh . . .*

I had fallen for the beginning of a gaslighting event and embarrassed myself.

The phone drama continued when Glen dropped Hunter off with me at my loft for the next transition. Glen said to me: "I am trying to help you because you are violating a restraining order by starting a long-term contract."

For Pete's sake! He was speaking to me as if I were a child who didn't understand and needed his "help." So condescending! And a restraining order for a phone contract is just asinine.

He then looked at Hunter and told him to go to his room and bring the phone box to him.

Hunter and I headed up to the loft. I looked outside about ten minutes later and the asshole was gone.

I am sure Glen's plan was to return the phone and take the money.

Glen called me after he left my home and said, "Bring me the box."

I replied, "I will not be giving you the box. Give me my phone so I can return it before the two-week period and cancel the contract. You can buy Hunter a phone if that is what you want."

Glen said in a threatening tone: "I am just trying to protect you and keep you out of trouble." *Click.* I called my lawyer to have him email Glen's attorney so I could return the phone.

Glen's attorney responded, "Glen dropped the phone off at Verizon."

I don't think my attorney forwarded my reply to Glen's lawyer, which read, *"Welcome to master level gaslighting. The phone is not at Verizon."*

Glen eventually gave the phone back to Hunter. The same endpoint was achieved, but with lots and lots of angst for Hunter and me.

Hunter was learning to deal with NPD.

❀

Glen would not give me the proof of insurance or updated vehicle registration for the Suburban, even though I had the vehicle at that time. I was not able to pay for the vehicle registration as Glen put vehicle titles under his name only. So when the registration expired, I had to park the vehicle. I parked it in a covered, public parking garage near my loft.

I went to California for a few days for work. During that time, Glen went to Maria and Jacob's house twice looking for the vehicle and asking if it was in their garage. Glen told Jacob he had a GPS tracker on the Suburban and he knew that I had been to their house at least twice.

Jacob said, "If you have a tracker on the Suburban, you should be able to locate it right now."

Glen told Jacob, "I have an agreement through the court that I am supposed to maintain the vehicles. The oil percentage is zero percent, so I need to get that taken care of."

I had never had the Suburban at their house, but I had the Jetta there twice. Creepy! I looked and was unable to find a tracker on my Jetta, but I suspect that it had already been removed.

Glen continued his search and eventually found the Suburban while I was still out of town. I had not hidden it intentionally. I mean, I would have done a much better job if this were my intent. It was parked in the parking garage next to my loft.

He emailed me a picture of the front passenger window, stating, *"The window was down and I reported it to the police in case something has been stolen out of my vehicle."*

I am not even sure if the window was down when I left it there. He had the other key, so . . . it was more likely that he had rolled it down for evidence that I was not caring for his vehicle.

The next day, I returned from California to find an empty spot where the Suburban had been parked. He had not informed me in the previous email that he had actually taken it.

Control regained for the NPD!

✿

Charles went to The House I Paid For to get his sweaters and his large Ziploc bags that he used for camping. Glen got home while Charles was loading his car and asked him what all he had taken from the house. Charles told him that he had taken his sweaters and the Ziploc bags. He then went into the house to get something else.

When Charles got back to the loft, where he was living with me for his college break, he found that the Ziploc bags were no longer in his car. His father had taken them, as I am sure he thought of them as his. We had to make a late-night run to the store to buy more bags because Charles was leaving for his camping trip the next morning.

So, I had moved out, finally, but the torment continued.

Chapter 36

Parenting Time

The parenting calendar and parenting time topic gets its own chapter because this was a source of fodder for Glen's harassment after the divorce was final. He had very little access to me anymore, so he clung to this connection with fervor.

When I initially moved out of The House I Paid For, the divorce was not final, and custody had not been determined. Therefore, it apparently had to be "fair" and we each had the kids every other week on a rotating schedule. This lack of control was driving Glen out of his mind, so he would change the calendar on a whim. I was never certain I would have the kids until they walked into the loft.

Eventually, the judge set an official schedule. This helped, but narcissists feel the rules don't apply to them, so they continue to do as they please.

Shortly after the judge made the ruling, Glen emailed me the calendar that he decided we would follow. This did not follow the rules set by the judge and there was no pattern that I could identify.

It took me a little while to figure this out, but the pattern was simply working around his hunting plans. I have always wanted the kids to have the ability to hunt with their dad, but not during my time with them, especially when I was not consulted as to how that might affect my plans. Also, as part of the schedule made by Glen, he had himself down for Thanksgiving and Christmas that year.

Glen was not happy when I did not agree to his foolish calendar. He left me a voicemail stating,

"I have 8-9 hunting and fishing trips planned with the boys through the end of this year, so I need the schedule that I proposed."

There were only thirteen weekends remaining in the proposed period, so he was unilaterally deciding to take some of my weekends.

The same day that I received this voicemail, Glen refused to meet me at Subway for the transition, so I dropped Hunter off at The House I Paid For. Glen was standing near the end of the driveway with our dog. The home is in the country and has a 200-yard gravel driveway. I drove past him to drop Hunter off at the house because he had three bags and because the judge did not agree with his rule that I was not able to drive up the driveway to drop the kids off at the house.

When I drove past Glen, he lunged toward the vehicle and hit the back of it with his hand. He did this intentionally to act as if he were hit by the back of the vehicle. He recorded me on video driving the rest of the way to the house, letting Hunter out, turning around and driving back down the driveway.

When I drove away, he texted, *"Not cool got it on video. It is not good to try and run me over on the driveway. I was standing in the driveway with Goldie very dangerous behavior."*

I was driving about five miles per hour and had made a clear path around him and the dog.

That night at 1:08 a.m., Glen called me and said, "If you don't accept my calendar, I am going to post that video."

I had a very hard time falling back asleep, as I was concerned about the welfare of the boys who were in his care when he had made that call. Glen was clearly decompensating.

My attorney informed me on a Friday that Glen filed a report with the police department. Glen's *modus operandi* was to create chaos on Fridays, for some mysterious reason. I suspect it was his attempt to ruin my weekend. In the report, he accused me of pushing him off a treadmill, just before moving from The House I Paid For. He also said I tried to run over him in the driveway when I dropped the kids off for his parenting time. A picture of a bruise on his leg was submitted as evidence.

The officer called my lawyer to let us know this was reported. He added that the report lacked credibility, but more specifics on that comment were not supplied.

I asked my attorney, "Will I be arrested? What should I do?"

He said he didn't think I would be arrested, but that I should leave my loft for the weekend. He said if I were arrested, I would remain in holding until Monday when the judge returned from the weekend. I was beside myself! I called Jenny and we decided I should stay at her house.

Nothing ever came of that filing, other than stress and wasted time.

❀

Glen would text me weekends he wanted to change. This was not in the form of a question but rather as a command starting with, *"I will have the kids . . ."*

Frequently his texts or emails became so abusive, and he was so unwilling to compromise that I would just refer him to my lawyer to work it out. I just couldn't expend the amount of energy required to deal with him.

After one such exchange in which I referred him to my lawyer, he responded, *"I'm sure it's very confusing for you to figure out where our kids can be you need help to do that I understand find another weekend"*

A demand and a comment about my stupidity, all in one interaction. Such efficient abuse! Really, he was so good at this!

❀

I was finally able to regain my financial footing and build a house. We moved out of the loft about six weeks before our house was ready. We lived in a hotel for four weeks and then with Jacob and Maria for three weeks during the final phases of the new build.

About the time we moved into the house, Glen sent an email to my lawyer stating I had been kicked out of the hotel.

Again, reading this information was bizarre! I knew this email was talking about me, but it was totally untrue and actually jaw-dropping.

Glen, in true NPD fashion, had created a convoluted cognitive distortion about me. He then sent it to someone who had the ability to make decisions about me and my ability to parent. What did it say? Why was I theoretically kicked out of the hotel? Drugs! He said I was selling drugs!

Of all the lies he could have come up with, that is probably the furthest from any possibility.

My lawyer smirked at me and asked if it was true. I said it was not. We both laughed at the audacity and that was the end of that story.

The harassment with the parenting schedule continued until our last child turned eighteen. Eventually, I just ignored his harsh comments. On the day Hunter turned eighteen, I blocked Glen from my phone.

Chapter 37

Medical Issues

One of the boys came to me and told me he was having trouble concentrating in school. We talked about how busy his week had been, with athletics events and classwork. He told me this was more than just being tired and busy and asked if he could go to the doctor.

I was so happy that he had this insight and that he was comfortable sharing his concerns with me and his doctor. I was also very worried and scared. I hated that he felt this turmoil.

The following day, I set up an appointment with his primary physician. I happened to see this physician while we were both doing rounds in the hospital. I gave him the short version of what was going on.

Then I emailed Glen that our son had an appointment with his doctor for problems with concentration. I told him the time, physician's name, and address. Glen was upset, stating I had switched their doctor. Our son had been seeing this doctor for at least three years, but Glen was out of touch with his children and insisted he see the pediatrician he had seen years prior.

In an attempt to control the situation, Glen canceled the appointment without telling me. Fortunately, the doctor called to let me know of this development. I told the doctor to make sure the appointment stayed in place, and I would guarantee that my son would be there.

This was very distressing on many levels.

After school, our son received a call from Glen telling him not to go to the appointment. He was forced to decide if he should listen to his mother or his father. I suspected this would be a concern, so I called him and told him this was not optional and that we were going to the appointment.

Glen did not show up for the appointment or ask either of us how it went.

Fortunately, this was a brief stress reaction in my child, and the potential crisis was averted.

I thank God for this doctor and his commitment to helping his patients.

One day, I was at work and received a voicemail from Glen saying, *"Sawyer has a humongous thyroid, and he needs to see a specialist. You should have been watching that better. He needs to see a specialist."*

Again, note the blame in this text. Why in the world would I be watching his thyroid? Also, note the crisis feeling in this text, which is typical of NPD.

There were multiple texts back and forth throughout the day.

I texted, *"I will have to look at Sawyer's neck tonight after he is done with work."*

Glen answered, *"You can check it on Friday"*

"If it is emergent enough to call me, I need to see it tonight."

"Non emergent"

"It is medical," I responded, *"and I need to see it tonight."*

"He has had it for a while you missed it"

"I need to see it tonight. What do you mean that I missed it? Isn't he your kid too."

"Relax Friday u can see him."

"I will see him tonight. He can come to my place or I will come to yours."

"Nope," Glen responded, with an additional message stating, *"Schedule a doctor appointment like the voice mail I left you and will getting there"*

"I need to see it. I am his mother."

"I got it if you make an appointment I'll make sure he gets her this week"

"I need to see this 'humungous mass' today."

"It's been like this for two weeks relax simmer down"

I called Sawyer and he said it was fine and no different that it had been for months. I had him send me a picture and it looked like normal thyroid cartilage, also known as an Adam's apple.

I asked Sawyer to meet me at the church across from The House I Paid For. I still wanted to look at it.

Unfortunately, Glen learned of our plan. As I was waiting at the church, Glen drove down the driveway toward me. As he drove by, he waved at me. He had Sawyer in the passenger seat. Sawyer looked at me and shrugged, indicating that he couldn't help what was happening.

He later told me that he had asked Glen to stop, but Glen wouldn't and told him, *"People are waiting for us to pick up a hay bale."* Glen called me just after they drove past me stating, *"We have plans."*

When I saw Sawyer later that week, his alleged throat ailment turned out to be nothing more than his perfectly normal Adam's apple.

In my studies, I learned that it is common behavior for people with NPD to walk, or drive in this case, away in the midst of a conversation to do something they deem as important and urgent.

The human brain and mind are fascinating!

Molly and I were in Maine, visiting Laura, during a time when I would be without my boys for ten days. I needed a distraction. These long stents were painful, as Glen would not allow me to see the kids at all during his time.

While I was in Maine, Glen had braces put on Hunter's teeth. I found out about this from a Facebook post!

After I saw this post on Facebook, I discovered an email from Glen, sent at 3:43 p.m. on the date the braces were placed, stating,

"Hunter has been evaluated for braces by the orthodontist, They have an opening today. He is very excited if all goes well he will have them off before Christmas his freshman year. I will have Hunter call you when he is done, he is so excited. I will send HSA reimbursement info in the near future."

A few weeks before that appointment, I had taken Hunter to his regular dentist, who told me to wait until Hunter was further into his growth cycle before considering braces. I had informed Glen of this appointment, but Glen opted not to attend. I also informed him of what the dentist recommended.

Note how he also tells me about the payment. We had not had an HSA (health savings account) for several years. When I reminded him of this, he told me to pay him for the braces, and he would pay the dentist. *The days of me just handing money to you are long gone, dude!* I am 100% convinced Glen had the braces placed on Hunter to get money from me.

Hunter knew I was upset, which made him feel like he had done something wrong. He worked through this in a conversation with Molly that same night. I called him, after learning he was troubled, and assured him I wasn't angry with him—but rather that Glen should have discussed this with me first.

Hunter felt guilty for not telling me, but he was stuck in the middle of this one.

The next day, I called the orthodontist office and learned the appointment was made about two weeks before the braces were placed. Glen had texted me that the date was moved up when someone else canceled. The orthodontist office confirmed that was not the truth.

The receptionist then asked for my phone number, as that information was blank on the initial paperwork. However, I was listed as the parent responsible for paying the bill. She also asked if I wanted to be listed as an emergency contact, because Glen and his brother were listed.

I sighed. "Yes, change his brother to me."

⚬

The kids and I lived in a renovated loft, which was cool and enhanced the downtown ambiance.

During one of the first nights, I saw a bat fly through my bedroom. I called animal control, but they were not able to locate the bat. I saw the bats again and noted that they burrowed into a hole in the brick wall of my bedroom. I called the manager of the loft, and they had a bat removal specialist secure the loft. I continued to see bats and called the manager multiple times. I was told they were probably the same bats that were now trapped.

I had animal control come a total of five times but only one bat was ever caught. That one tested negative for rabies. I did some reading and learned that the rabies series of shots was required if you ever awoke with a bat in your room. This is because you may not feel, or see, a bite. At this same time, Hunter showed me a couple little spots at the base of his neck in the back. I looked up the Centers for Disease Control (CDC) website and learned the shots are necessary before any rabies symptoms occur or "the disease is nearly always fatal."[2] I contacted an infectious disease doctor and set up an appointment.

Of course, we all had to get the full rabies series. As soon as I learned that the shots were required, I emailed Glen with all the information. He received this email a full twenty-four hours before our appointment to start the series. The three oldest kids, no longer minors, were able to get their shots without incident.

When I was with Hunter at our appointment for the first set of shots, Glen called the medical office and yelled at the receptionist that he "forbid" them from giving the shots to Hunter. The doctor came into the exam room and asked me to meet him in the hall. He told me what was transpiring. He told me he was going ahead with the shot series anyway, as he had already reported the case to the CDC and was now required, by the state, to give Hunter the series. With a sympathetic expression, he said, "I am just letting you know what is happening."

That whole incident was stressful! And I was embarrassed that my former spouse had behaved that way to a colleague.

Gives Me Bits of Information

Glen frequently left out important facts.

In 1994, shortly after I gave birth to Molly, Glen told me he was going to be working out of state for two weeks. This was when I was busy as a chief resident.

Glen nonchalantly told me before he left that a college friend was going to stay at our house for a few days. This friend was starting a new job near where we lived, and Glen told me that he needed a place to stay while he looked for a house.

This was a man, and not someone I knew!

The friend showed up, with his wife, toddler son, teenage son, a dog and his mother, who had a chronic cough from emphysema. Their little, yippy dog that was an indoor dog. We had a dog too, but she was an outdoor dog.

This family was very nice and appreciative. I am certain they thought I had been involved in the plan. The plan was not for one person to stay at our house while the realtor helped him find a house, but was for this entire family to move into our house until they could find a house. This was what Glen had invited them to do, without telling me.

They stayed for five weeks! Glen was out of town this entire time, as his two-week trip somehow extended to five weeks.

Glen got all the credit while I did all the work. All while breastfeeding an infant in my bedroom as there were no longer any private spaces in our small house.

Chapter 39

Safety

Several years before I decided to file for divorce, I noticed small, brief muscle twitches in my arms and legs. These are called fasciculations. We have probably all experienced these around our eyes when we are over tired or have had too much caffeine. They ordinarily last a day or two, but mine were all over and lasted several weeks.

My neurology brain immediately kicked into overdrive. To say I was in a panic situation would be a gross understatement, as fasciculations are a sign of possible ALS (amyotrophic lateral sclerosis), also called Lou Gehrig's disease.

I noticed the fasciculations shortly after I laid down to go to sleep for the night. I was alone, as was routine at this point in our marriage since Glen usually fell asleep on the couch, would come to bed for a couple hours in the middle of the night, and then be gone before I awoke. I cried all night, thinking Hunter would only be in third grade when I died, after becoming too weak to walk and eventually becoming ventilator-dependent.

Knowledge was my power and my nemesis!

At 7:30 the next morning, Jenny called me.

I answered with a short, "Hi."

"What is wrong?" she asked.

"I have ALS," I said with a matter-of-fact tone. She asked me why I thought this, and we talked through my symptoms. She is a specialist in neurophysiology, which includes ALS and the testing for it. Yes, I have the absolute best friends!

She said, "Come to the office now and I will test you."

The test did not show ALS! Thank the Lord! I would be able to raise my kids.

We talked through the options for the diagnosis and checked labs that were also normal. She did a neurologic exam that was also normal except for the obvious continued fasciculations.

During this time, I also felt slightly off balance.

Jenny suggested that I investigate whether any chemicals had been used at our house in case I had been exposed to a pesticide or some other toxin. I asked Glen and he said he had not used anything. Laura was married to a toxicologist, so I spoke with him. He said the over-the-counter chemicals that a layperson could get ahold of were not strong enough to do this. He added that someone would need a license to buy anything strong enough to cause fasciculations.

Glen had worked for a company that sprayed for flies and other bugs previously, and he kept that license.

A few days later, we were getting into the car for church. One of our kittens was near the vehicle, so I took my foot and gently directed the kitten away from the tire. The kitten fell over. She got up to walk and was very unsteady, nearly falling over.

Glen started laughing.

I said, "It is not funny. Something is wrong with her."

I picked up the kitty and felt her fasciculations. Pieces were coming together at this point.

I told Glen we needed to see what the kitty and I had been exposed to. That we needed to check the chemicals that we owned and learn if any of those could be the culprit.

He said, "What, do you think I poisoned you?"

Let that statement sit for a bit. The realization that I had been poisoned is still a hard one to settle many years later. *Someone intentionally tried to harm me! I am the mother of his children for cripes' sakes!* I use that phrase because the words I really feel are too harsh for this book.

I am certain that I ingested that poison in a latte.

Shortly before the fasciculations started, I awoke one morning to find a latte on my nightstand. It was from Glen.

I had a fleeting, insane thought: *Maybe I can work harder and make this marriage work.*

I took a sip and thought the hazelnut syrup had artificial sweeteners as it tasted slightly off. I drank about half of it.

༄

The next safety issue occurred after I had filed for divorce, but before I was allowed to move out of our house. It was the dead of winter in snowy South Dakota when my mother noticed 150 pounds of bagged sand in the trunk of my car. This is commonly done in the winter to add weight to your vehicle and lessen the chance of sliding on icy roads.

She exclaimed, "You can't have extra weight in the trunk of a front-wheel drive vehicle in the winter!"

I had wondered why my car was handling poorly on the ice that year, but simply thought that I needed new tires.

When my mom asked Sawyer to help her remove them, he said, "I told Dad not to put those in Mom's car."

Why would he do this? I now understood that he would definitely hurt me, but the kids also rode in that car. A narcissist only loves himself!

I always worried when the kids rode with Glen because he had no regard for speed limits. Recall, the rules don't apply to narcissists. I was even more concerned if they were at any event that potentially involved alcohol.

Shortly after the divorce was final, all the kids rode with Glen to a family wedding in a town about one hour away from The House I Paid For. I found out from the kids that Glen had Hunter, then age sixteen, drive them all home from the event. That part is fine, as Glen had been drinking.

The problem came in the details. Glen wanted Hunter to drive a different route for an unknown, and unexplained, reason. Hunter was driving on the highway, at highway speed, as they were passing the turn that Glen preferred. Glen grabbed the wheel to start to turn on this preferred route! Our son-in-law yelled for Glen to stop, while my own kids were frozen in their learned response of avoiding confrontation with Glen.

Chapter 40

Post Separation Abuse

A few weeks after I filed for divorce, Glen called me on my way to work.

He told me, "Put money into our joint checking account to pay me back for the bills I have paid in the last forty days."

By this time, I had gained control of my earnings. I said, "All income is marital income, and it is appropriate that you pay some bills. I am not responsible for everything. Give me any additional bills and I will pay them directly."

He responded, "I have always paid the bills, and I will keep doing it. You owe me for bills that I paid with my own money."

I reiterated, "All income is marital income, and I will not be writing a check to you."

A few days later, I was at a neuroscience conference before starting my morning clinic.

Glen called and said, "If you don't bring a $54,000 check to me at work by noon, a moving company is going to pack up your stuff to move it out by 4 p.m.today."

I answered, "I am not writing you a check for family bills."

He called me at noon and asked if I was going to bring the check.

I told him again, "I am not writing you a check for family bills."

He texted me at 12:07 p.m.: *"I guess that is a no."*

This was an empty threat, but I worried about it all day.

Also, the amount of money he was asking for was an insane sum for forty days of bills. Despite my asking, he did not tell me specifically what this was for. I do not know where he came up with this number. I am sure it was not for bills, and I suspect it was something he owed money for that I was not supposed to know about. He bought things without my knowledge all the time.

⚘

While we still lived together, Glen started opening my mail before he gave it to me.

When I told him not to do this, he said, "It is addressed to my house. I am paying the bills, so it is my house. You can leave."

Glen did have a job by this point, but I had paid for the overwhelming majority of the house. He wrote the checks for the bills, as I didn't have access to our money, but he paid with money that, again, was mostly earned by me.

His distorted thought processes concluded that he paid the bills, so the house was his.

One morning, I was getting ready to leave for work when a typed note slid under my bathroom door. It said that I needed to pay $54,000 to Glen.

Sigh! What is the deal with this dollar amount? And I had told him several times to give me all the bills. To that point, he had not given me any.

The note said that he had taken out a loan to pay the bills and that I also now owed him $1,000 in interest.

I brought the letter to my lawyer, who contacted Glen's lawyer to have him stop the harassment.

This is all gaslighting, so don't feel like you should have made sense of the whole incident around the $54,000. I am certain that this was simply to get money from me.

❀

One day, Glen texted me at work asking, *"Where is check book ? I need to write checks for healthcare coverage."*

I responded, *"I don't know where your checkbook is. I already paid for the next 6 months of health insurance."*

Health insurance and medical bills were the only bills I had always paid, as all other financial matters were managed by Glen.

Later that morning, he texted, *"I paid the bill as they called me that it was due."*

I called the insurance company, and the agent told me there was nothing due because they had already received my check. I asked if she had spoken with Glen, and she said she had not. She told me that they would not have called until the bill was past due, which it was not.

I asked Glen, "When did you speak with them?"

He stated, "It is none of your business. I already paid it. I won. Now you need to reimburse me."

Again, he was just trying to get me to give him money.

In total, I received eighteen texts regarding this issue over a four-hour period while I was at work.

Several days later, Glen called me at work, asking, "What is your Visa credit card number?"

What I wanted to text was, *"Okay, dumbass! I think we have established that I am not giving financial control back over to you!"* Instead, I responded, *"I am not giving that to you."*

He responded: *"I need the number because we have 5 or 6 accounts open under our names."*

I replied, *"The card I have is under my name alone."*

Glen said, *"I can't close them then, so any fees will be yours to pay."*

He also asked Charles for his personal credit card number that same day. Charles wouldn't give it to him either.

Again, this is gaslighting, so that is why this whole thing makes no sense.

With that same text exchange, I informed Glen that I had taken my name off our only shared credit card. I told him the card would be inactive for a few days until he filled out paperwork that the credit card company would send him.

A few days later, he asked, "What did you do with the credit card? It is not working."

I repeated, "It is inactive until you fill out the paperwork. I told you about this."

"Call Visa and reinstate the card," he demanded. He hung up on me and then called me seven times in rapid succession because I did not answer to allow him to further abuse me.

He then texted, *"The power has shut off because of the credit card issue."*

Later that day, he doubled down by texting, *"I have reservations for the family inn tomorrow. We cannot stay here without power. Thanks. Children's family inn sounds like a fun week."*

I called the energy company and spoke with a representative. She said the power had not been shut off and had never been shut off. She said there was no overdue charge.

✿

Another time, I received a call from the financial planner that assisted with the children's 529 plans (tax-advantaged investment accounts designed to help families save for a child's future education expenses). He told me that Molly and Charles had both called him to pay their tuition for that semester because it was due.

Glen was the executor of the 529s, so his approval was needed before any funds were released. Oddly, those plans could only have one executor, and of course it was Glen.

Anyway, Glen was refusing to release the funds. Instead, he wanted the money sent directly to him. He told the financial planner that he would then write a check to the colleges. The financial planner told me that this could legally be done this way, but that it is more efficient to directly send money from the 529 to the college. He said the kids had told him the tuition was due the next day, so time was of the essence.

The financial planner called Glen again and then called me stating, "It didn't go well," and that Glen still refused to allow the funds to go directly to the college accounts.

I texted Glen: *"The college tuition is due tomorrow for Molly and Charles. You need to allow the direct transfer of the money from the 529 plans to the colleges or there will be a late fee."*

He responded, *"Why would you withhold that information till the last hour the last day and it's a busy Friday at work for me you know that"*

Meanwhile, he was texting Molly at the same time, stating he was on the way to a football game, so I knew he was available to address this.

I texted back: *"The kids have been telling you this repeatedly for the last week. The financial planner told you this at least 3 times as well."*

"I am not aware of the situation"

Molly ended up paying her tuition from her savings; she had a part-time job and had been saving money for a study abroad semester.

When she called him to discuss the repayment to her from the 529, he told her I was using her to get money out of the 529, and told her that is illegal.

He called her later and told her, "The financial planner said they can't take money out of the account when it is a payment from the past. Because your parents have paid so much of your college tuition already, we can't go back in time and repay you for tuition."

He texted her later that evening, *"Molly I'm the one that's looking out for your best financial interest in the future please trust me."*

❀

Another time, Glen emailed me:

"I am purchasing a new trailer for you and me both to support the kids mowing business. I found a great deal from out neighbor."

He continued: *"I will hope that tis will provide you with the confidence to begin pulling trailers with mowers to assist in the kids business and income. I will be available at any time to you, and me I will store it at the house and we both will pay for it."*

This lawn mowing service was a job with two clients.

I responded,

"We have 2 trailers, so they can use those"

Additionally, I have been driving pickup trucks with horse trailers since I was fourteen years old. My confidence in this was just fine.

❀

One year after I filed for divorce, but before it was settled, I discovered that Glen was listed as the beneficiary for all our children's life insurance policies. We had previously both been listed. He had his brother listed as a contingency. Glen had also changed his personal life insurance beneficiary from me to his brother.

We had both been instructed by the judge not to change any beneficiaries until the divorce was settled.

Meanwhile, as a rule follower by nature, I still had Glen as the sole beneficiary on my life insurance policy, until one hour after the divorce papers were signed. I changed the beneficiary on the children's plans at that time as well.

Glen was like a malignant tumor in my brain, and I was slowly extricating the tumor, one tendril at a time.

Chapter 41

Rules Don't Apply

Narcissists do not think rules apply to them. They feel entitled to break rules, as those are boundaries set for the common man, not them. Not for someone with a distorted, grandiose sense of self.

I had several incidents throughout my marriage and divorce process, as well as throughout the time we had minor children, in which Glen would apply rules to me, but those same rules did not apply to him.

Glen would not allow the kids to go to the traditional family Christmas for my side of the family when it landed during his parenting time. It had to be a prolonged back-and-forth text exchange for me to get that time. However, he would call every hunting trip a "family reunion" and simply dictated that as a tradition in which the kids would be with him, no matter which parent was on the parenting schedule.

Our attorneys informed us that neither parent could take the children out of state without the other's permission. I followed this rule, even when I was taking the two minor children to see their older siblings in Nebraska and Minnesota.

Glen didn't follow this rule, and it was not enforced. It seemed that some divorce rules and laws were simply put in place to make you look petty when you reported it to your lawyer. Those rules seem only made for those who will follow them.

Here's an example. Someone on Glen's side of the family in Kansas had a wedding. Glen never informed me of the plan, but I knew the wedding was that weekend. On a Thursday evening, I received a text from Hunter discussing a fish. I realized he was already in Kansas. This meant that Hunter and Sawyer had been taken out of state without my permission, and they were missing two days of school without my knowledge.

Glen texted me the next Monday morning, after returning from the trip, stating, *"Sawyer and Haunter and Glen are going to the wedding for the weekend we will be back on Monday the boys will drive into the apartment and see you Monday at five we will cross multiple state lines going to and from."*

As a reminder, I leave Glen's quotes exactly as said, texted or emailed. They all required a high level of interpretation, and he frequently spelled Hunter's name wrong.

Glen's written communication was like the "Magic Eye" puzzles in the newspaper. Those are the pictures of multiple dots that you have to stare at and cross your eyes until a 3D image eventually appears.

So, at this point, I also learned that the kids were missing school on Monday as well.

When I confronted Glen about breaking the rules, he did his usual gaslighting that is hard to follow.

He texted, *"I let you know six times that I asked for the suburban to go to the wedding this weekend with the kids and you denied access."*

Sawyer called and let me know he had cross country practice but would head to the loft when that was done. I told him this was fine.

Glen heard Sawyer talking to me on the phone and texted, *"Please do not be so hard on the kids when it comes to change times they want to relax after cross country visit with their friends and not be pressured to drive hundred miles an hour back-and-forth to meet your time Needs for transition."*

❀

On the advice of my lawyer, I rented a new post office box where I would receive their communications and my other mail.

Glen somehow figured out where I had this box, even though it was not at our local post office. He then went to this post office and filled out a form that redirected my mail from my new P.O. box to his new P.O. box. His name was not on my box and my name was not on his, yet the post office staff complied with his request and had my mail diverted to him!

That is so messed up! I can't fathom how anyone thought that was okay! And he did this three times!

When I confronted Glen about redirecting my mail, he replied, "I have a PO Box? Do you have a PO Box? Where is my mail?"

He later texted, *"I do not have or care to have your mail."*

Wow, that is a lot of work for someone who doesn't even want my mail.

I thought, *How in the hell did I marry this idiot loser?*

I was originally alerted to the P.O. box hijacking when I received an email from the postmaster at the post office where Glen had his box.

She told me there were "some red flags" because my mail was being forwarded to Glen. I went to my post office and the supervisor showed me a form that Glen had signed. They would not give me a copy because of "confidentiality" for Glen!

Through gritted teeth I said, "So you weren't worried about MY privacy when you literally gave him my private mail, but now HE has the right of privacy?"

I was so flabbergasted that I just walked out. There was nothing more to say when someone answered without basic logic.

I called the postmaster general, and he said he couldn't do anything because it was a "civil matter."

I said, "How about you follow federal law and charge him with stealing mail?"

I was so frustrated with this lack of control over my own mail! It was a very defeating moment. Everyone seemed to be helping Glen continue to have control over me simply because we were married. This is the patriarchal society we live in.

One morning when I awoke, my first thought was that I had accidentally hung my keys on the hook by the door. This was automatic, as I had hung my keys in that spot for several years before divorce proceedings had begun.

I thought, *Oh no, my post office key is on there*. I went downstairs and as predicted, the keys were there but the post office key was gone. I went to the post office and paid the fee to change the lock.

So, messing with my mail was breaking federal law. But. Nobody. Gave. A. Shit!!! I was on my own to extract myself from this criminal as soon as possible, with as minimal harm as possible.

Chapter 42

The Pool

Ultimately, it was decided that I would be "awarded" my business and Glen would get the marital home. This was fine in the sense that I didn't think I would ever feel safe living in that home, where I would need to change all the locks and search for hidden cameras.

But, and this is a big ass but, I had been the only one contributing to the payment of that house for eleven of the fifteen years that I lived there! I had been working and therefore away from my kids to pay that mortgage. Fine!

So, I say that I was fine with this decision, but I will qualify by saying, I was not fine with relinquishing the pool. When Shon died, I had a really hard time concentrating for a full year. This was through my entire second year of medical school. It was a very hard and very sad time. And I was only twenty-three years old. Anyway, during a particularly hard week, I finished a microbiology exam and handed it in.

I walked out the doors of the medical school and sat on the steps. I decided this was simply too much and I needed to take a year off. I just couldn't do it! I needed a break! Maybe I would quit altogether, but I would make that decision during my year off. My friends, who had been by my side through this horror, found me sitting on the steps. The three of them listened to me, through my tears, explaining my decision.

One of them said, "But you have always wanted a pool. You have always said you can get through medical school because you want a pool."

We all sat with that for a couple minutes. We talked more about how they would help me study and they would remain by my side through this. Ultimately, I decided I would keep going. Partly because of the pool, but mostly because I didn't think I could do it later without my classmates—all of them.

So, the pool represented my grit and perseverance. I stayed in school. I studied hard. I passed all the exams. I worked to make money to pay for it. It was mine and it was ripped from me!

My kids know I do not want any discussion of the pool at my house. I don't want to know when it opens for the season, when they are in it, when they hang out with their friends in it, any of it. This is still a gut check for me. Would I take back my prior life for it? Absolutely not! But it is not right that my abuser is still able to enjoy it.

✲

Chapter 43

The Divorce Process

It is interesting to take an honest look at your life. A bird's eye view of how it has turned out thus far, set against the backdrop of your hopes and dreams. To decide if you have lived anything close to the life you desire. The life you deserve.

I took that look, and didn't like what I saw. I needed more. I needed safety and security. I needed to control my destiny. I needed someone to hold me up and have my back. I needed someone to love me. I needed a divorce!

As I took this critical look at my life, my journal kept the score as I summed up the marriage:

"I have been taken advantage of and betrayed throughout this marriage. Our marriage is not an equal partnership. Glen takes much more from it, and I contribute much more to it. I

have been the primary breadwinner and caregiver. I also maintain the household.

Glen is a frivolous spender and always buys things in excess, often without consulting, or even informing, me. I have always been frugal and put my needs and wants behind those of my family.

I have attempted to provide financial security for myself and my family. I thought I had done this, but I was betrayed, not only by Glen's irresponsible spending, but by his withholding of financial information. Glen has put our family's financial security in ruins, possibly to the point of being irreparable in my lifetime. This is not a position that I should have been forced into, given the choices I have made and the work I have done.

I am the victim of severe emotional abuse secondary to intentional manipulation from a person with a pattern of extreme behaviors. It is not my responsibility, nor is it in my power, to change Glen's dysfunctional behavior patterns.

I have to leave.

The first step in divorce is finding the right lawyer. My friend, since preschool, is a divorce attorney. We decided it was best if she was not the one to represent me, as our friendship was more important than the outcome of my divorce. She told me who to hire and talked me through the process. I knew that whomever she recommended could be trusted, and I needed to trust completely as my life was in their hands. Also, the overview of the process helped me know what to expect. I am a girl who loves a plan!

To be fully transparent, this was not our original plan. The original plan was to marry 1970s TV stars Leif Garrett and Shaun Cassidy, live together on a horse farm in Hawaii, and work as a pediatrician and a veterinarian. But, yeah, we at least had a plan.

At my first meeting with the lawyer, I was asked a series of questions. One question pertained to the reason for the divorce.

I answered, "I am done with this charade. Glen is a narcissist and as such, he is unable to maintain long-term relationships. The relationship is doomed."

Black and white, no gray to be seen, the divorce was required, and I had come to terms with that. I had already stayed as long as I could.

But my black and white answer was not on the surprisingly short list of options, so I settled on "irreconcilable differences." That did not come anywhere close to describing why I was filing, but that was the square option that fit the best in the round hole.

As I started to read about divorce, I learned you are supposed to explain patterns of behavior rather than apply your opinion on a diagnosis. However, having spent years observing Glen's behavior and being board certified with the American Academy of Psychiatry and Neurology, I can't unknow what I know. With all due respect, that is my opinion on a diagnosis, Your Honor.

⚘

The divorce process is incredibly intrusive. Your privacy is gone. You are required to provide detailed financial and medical records. You fill out interrogatories about the most private aspects of your life.

An appraiser comes and makes a record of, and attaches a cost to, all your material items, including your house, your property, and, well, all of your stuff.

You meet with your lawyer and provide intimate details about your married life that you have not shared with anyone but your closest friend.

⚜

One day, I was instructed to provide my password for my Facebook account, per a request from Glen's lawyer. Shortly after providing this, I received a message on Facebook from Glen, instructing me to delete a picture that was on my Facebook account. I had already blocked him from my Facebook, so the only way he was able to see these pictures was with the use of my password. I changed the password immediately and told my lawyer that I would not be supplying passwords again.

I am in dumbfounded awe that a lawyer would request this. Can you imagine what an NPD could post to get me in trouble?

⚜

During the divorce process, my main goal was to secure primary physical and legal custody of the minor children. The ability to control your future, and therefore your children's future, lies in the hands of a human, a judge. I know what is best for my kids, yet someone else, a stranger, was left to make the "best" decision for them.

⚜

The divorce process is a savage, sanctioned, vilification process. Lawyers are hired to make the opposing party look bad. It is literally their job in this scenario.

Glen's lawyer understood the assignment and approached

it with gusto. The ability to bully and gaslight me was essentially transferred from Glen to his lawyer. His lawyer became his "flying monkey," his well-paid lackey who he used to do his bidding. It was surreal to read emails about myself that were total, confabulated bullshit. I would read these emails that described a raging, unfit mother and think, *This is about me? None of this is true!* But it went on and on.

Eventually my armor was chipped away, and I couldn't help but wonder if maybe what the attorney was saying was true. I would have to step back, with a larger lens, and remind myself that this was all lies. But these lies could affect the outcome of the divorce, and therefore significantly affect my life and the lives of my children. I felt helpless to control my own destiny because the reality was that I could not control my destiny. I had to trust a very broken system.

Fortunately, I had fantastic lawyers who would call this what it was: total, meritless crap. They believed in me and defended me, but it all rested on a judge who could not know the complexity that was me and my family.

⚜

Fortunately, the divorce was finalized in mediation, with a retired judge who listened intently. We had two full days for him to hear both of our sides. I was finally feeling heard, but it is hard to briefly summarize more than twenty years of abuse.

Suddenly, it was over, after fifteen long months. The money and material items were split. I was awarded what was determined to be my share of custody of the minor children. It is just bizarre to be "awarded" custody of your own children.

The children I grew in my body, gave birth to, breast fed, cared for when they were sick, and generally kept alive and thriving. Thank you so much for awarding me something that was always mine!

My lawyer made certain I had someone to accompany me from the proceedings to my apartment, as there is an increased risk of physical harm from a narcissist at that time.

People with NPD find the legal battle to be a forum for placing the blame on the other person and they feel validated that their lawyer listened to their allegations that the other person is "all bad." Additionally, the narcissist's persona has taken a hit since someone publicly chose to leave them. That is very threatening to their fragile ego. Glen suffered a huge narcissistic injury, and I needed to be careful.

Fortunately, Jenny was already parked outside waiting to take me home.

Meanwhile, I looked at my fatherly lawyer and asked, "Now what do I do?"

My life had gone from abuse to the all-encompassing legal battle. My life had been on hold for so long.

He answered, "You just live."

I sighed, "Just live? I am not sure I know how to do that anymore."

It sounds so simple, but to me, it was a foreign concept.

I decided at that moment that I was going to make my life great. I was getting a do-over and would enter it with open eyes. Open, experienced eyes, brain, and heart. I decided to do this right! I had survived a marriage with a cloud over my head, weathered the thunderstorm that is divorce, and emerged into a freshly washed field of sunshine and wildflowers. My painful past was behind me, and a hopeful future was before me.

After the papers were signed, I went outside to join Jenny. It was a moment of pure joy between two friends who had been through so much together. We were coincidentally both going through divorce at the same time. We had struggled together, cried together, counseled each other, read and discussed books about narcissists and divorce together. Most importantly, we unconditionally supported each other. And we eventually both made it to the other side.

Chapter 44

Stolen Ability to Be Vulnerable

Glen stole my ability to be vulnerable. My confidence had slowly eroded with the years of gaslighting and other abuse. This made it difficult for me to trust myself and my decisions.

It took me years to decide to go through with the divorce. Once I successfully navigated those treacherous waters, I was able to keep taking steps forward. I slowly gained independence and confidence.

I kept reminding myself that each thing I accomplished brought me one step closer to a better life. I did not know how many steps that would take, but I was one step closer.

At the end of 2016, as I was overwhelmed with what I still needed to do, I made a list of my accomplishments from that year alone. I was surprised at what I had already done.

Here is the actual list:

- Ran 4th marathon

- Organized finances, investments, and insurance

- Organized stuff for filing taxes

- Changed back to maiden name

- Bought new car – paid in full

- Sold my business

- Obtained mortgage for new home

- Planned new home from layout to decor

- Paid for full year of college for 2 kids

- Made new will, trust, living will and assigned a power

  of attorney

- Traveled to Ireland

- Filed contempt charge

Chapter 45

Wrap It All Up

When I was finally able to write the last check to my abuser, five years after the divorce, I dropped it off at my attorney's office per protocol. The attorney contacted Glen that the check was ready. After several failed attempts, Glen finally responded; however, he waited several weeks to pick it up. This was odd, as he had picked up all the prior checks and cashed them immediately. I don't have an explanation for this, other than the fact that this really ended any connection and control over me.

Glen needed to sign the Final Satisfaction so this could be filed with the court as proof that my obligation was complete.

I advised my lawyer that Glen should sign the form before the check was handed over. This information was given to the front receptionist, and a sticky note was placed on the check. As is my luck with all that involves Glen, there was a new receptionist when Glen came to the office. He asked for the check, and it was handed across the desk. Somehow the sticky note was missing.

The receptionist told him he needed to sign the final paperwork. Glen said he could not see without his glasses and needed to go out to his vehicle to get them. He took the check and walked out, got in his vehicle and drove away. The receptionist was waving him down from the doorway as he pulled out of the parking lot.

He cashed the check but would not return my lawyer's call to come back and sign the Final Satisfaction. Eventually, Glen was summoned to court to sign in front of the judge. In true narcissistic fashion, rules don't apply, and he did not show up in court! He simply did not show up or even correspond in any fashion.

The judge ruled that the case was concluded with the act of cashing the check. Really? No shit?! But let's have the man, my abuser, sign off and say the divorce process was complete. For crying out loud, this process is so messed up!

Misogyny is defined as the ingrained prejudice against women. The prefix "mis" means false or against, and "gyn" means woman or female. What happened to me with this court scenario is misogyny.

Deep, cleansing breath for me at this point, though: I was finally completely free! However, I would have loved to state my discontent to the judge. Just to speak my female voice and let him know I am a smart, strong, independent woman and

I did not appreciate the inherent bias in this entire process. I certainly did not need or appreciate the fact that Glen had the final say that I was completely free.

Chapter 46

Continued Harassment After Divorce Is Final

In my fantasies, or delusions, while awaiting the completion of the divorce, life was to become immediately easier after the divorce was final. That was true in several respects, but we still had to co-parent for a few years. This is better known as parallel parenting when dealing with a character such as Glen. We were both parenting per our own style and rules, with limited communication with each other. At least limited constructive communication.

We had a Parent Coordinator (PC) to assist with enforcing the judge's rules regarding the parenting calendar. They are supposed to make each decision based on the best interest of the children. The PC has the legal ability to make decisions on the fly without consulting the judge or any lawyers.

Sounds good, right? But remember that one part of my equation was an NPD. The PC needed to understand, really understand, NPD and they also needed to possess the gonads (testes or ovaries) to stand up to the NPD. My PC was a psychologist, so you would think this would make him the perfect candidate. Nope! He had no nuts! Zero!

An interesting fact of divorce is that both parents will fall into the same category. The way one parent acts is the way you are both presumed to act. No individualization. No learning who we both were. We were both treated as the difficult one. So, I was on my own to navigate and deal with parenting with Glen. In fact, it was worse than that as Glen could send our PC down long rabbit holes trying to determine who was being truthful and who was lying. And this time, I was negotiating with someone who had a major narcissistic injury, so he wanted, needed, to get back at me and put me in my place.

The first issue came one month after the divorce was final. I knew it wouldn't take long. Narcissists are nothing if not predictable!

It was a Sunday, and I was flying home from a speaking engagement for my research. It was not my parenting time until Monday after school, so I was on my own. Glen left a voicemail, at 10 a.m. on Sunday, stating he was leaving town for work, so I needed to take the kids that night. Sawyer was seventeen and Hunter was thirteen at this time.

I received this voicemail message when I landed in Chicago at 2 p.m. I called Glen and he did not answer.

I called Sawyer and he said the plan was for Hunter to go

to Glen's parents' house until he could pick him up about 9:30 p.m. They were then going to come to my house, as he knew I would be home by that time.

Glen then called saying, "I have sacrificed for the last three nights and now I need to leave for work."

I responded, "You didn't inform me of any calendar change, but I will be home tonight, so it is fine."

Glen called me again, shouting, "The boys are just about to your apartment. Where is the key?"

He hung up on me as I was repeating what Sawyer had described as the plan.

I called Sawyer and he said they were just about to Grandma's house and the plan had not changed.

Glen texted:

"I talked to grandma Kay if you don't want to take care of Sawyer and Hunter for a few nights they"ll take care of him until you're comfortable with seeing them again."

He continued: *"Try to be a better parent is all I'm asking . . . if work calls for you to be away you know I love take care the cats I'll take care of them never a problem with me to take care of my kids".*

This is gaslighting! He was the one leaving for work during his parenting time.

⚜

I put this next gaslighting incident into a bullet point timeline, as it is very prolonged. Journaling was my savior for these events because it enabled me to keep track of facts and keep the focus on the actual issue at hand.

Timeline of acquiring my material items after divorce finalized December 2, 2015:

December 11: I got very little in the way of material assets as I was basically "awarded" my business, one ATV and my old, manual Jetta. I did have a few things at The House I Paid For that I needed to retrieve.

> I contacted Glen asking him to supply dates for movers to pick up my stuff.
>
> He texted, *"my lawyer will send proposed dates for transfer It may take up to 90 days once all the other transactions are completed."*

January 20: I texted, *"I will schedule someone to pick up my stuff in the next 2 weeks. What date works for you?"*

No reply.

January 26: I reminded him again that I still needed a few dates.

He texted back, *"Nope."*

January 27: I texted, *"I will have someone get my stuff Feb 19 or 20."*

> He responded *"You can get it January 28. The furniture is ready to go in the enclosed deck. I have 90 days to get the rest ready to go."*
>
> There is actually no enclosed deck, so it was simply out in the snowy winter elements. I responded, *"I will let my lawyer know my furniture is outside."*

He responded *"It is safe and dry , relax. U have 2 days to pick items up."*

The ninety-day timeline was his message to me that he was not releasing my stuff to me until I completed my obligations to him, one of which was financial and would legally take ninety days to complete.

January 29: To prevent weather damage, I had to act quickly. I had Sawyer and his friends move my stuff to Jacob and Maria's shed. Sawyer also drove my ATV to their shed, as that was also part of my division of assets.

January 30: The next morning, Glen showed up unannounced at Jacob and Maria's house and insisted they give him the keys to my ATV. He told them it was his to keep until April 26. This was not true, but he made this up to fit the narrative he desired. Maria refused to give him the keys and Glen threatened to call the sheriff. He left to go find his other set of keys.

> Glen texted me, *"I did not give you permission to take the ATV from the house I will arrange dates when you can come and take things from the house stop stealing things from the house."*

Jacob started calling storage businesses and found one that could take my items the next day.

While Jacob was on the phone regarding the storage unit, he looked out the window and saw that Glen had returned to their shed. Glen trespassed into their storage shed and drove off with my ATV.

I called the deputy and told him I wanted to file charges. He came to discuss this with me, and I shared the details. He then went to get a statement from Glen.

The deputy later informed me that Glen said, "We are no longer working with lawyers because we both agreed that the divorce decree documents were not correct. We were not going to go through the lawyers as it would cost money, and it would make the lawyers look stupid." He also told the deputy that he had the ATV for ninety more days.

The deputy told Glen to have the ATV back to the shed by noon.

Why were there no charges filed, we all ask? Because "this is a civil matter." Unfortunately, this was not the end of the problem as I still had not gotten several other items from The House I Paid For.

May: I texted Glen multiple times to coordinate a date, to pick up the rest of my material items, but to no avail. It took him five months to respond to my question at all, and he only responded at that time because I asked him if I needed to contact his lawyer to force him to pick a date.

He answered, *"I don't have a lawyer our divorce was over in December remember"* and then *"If you cannot return my personal items this message confirms that we are done transferring any other divorce items as of May 18th 1 PM"*

I had very few items of his as I was the one that moved out with only a small list of approved items. I had his wedding ring and a cookbook his mother had given me as a gift. Those items were not listed in the divorce documents, so technically I didn't need to give them to him. I was keeping the wedding ring mostly to piss him off anyway. The day I asked for the divorce, he put his ring by my sink. I think he did this as a statement of finality or something. I picked it up and thought, *fine, I will keep this and sell it.*

July 20: I emailed Glen, again asking him to pick a date for the movers to come.

July 30: He responded, *"August 15th is the only date in the near future that will work to pick up items that are listed in the Divorce Decree to pick up."*

He later added, *"Your additional request of items is denied those are not in the divorce decree in the affidavit"*

I don't even know what he was talking about with this one as I had not requested anything other than the things awarded to me and clearly spelled out in the paperwork. I think he was trying to make a case that I was requesting other things, or else he was drunk.

August 6: I arranged movers for August fifteenth, as Glen had picked this particular day. I hired a representative to bring the documents that included the list of items to be retrieved. I was not able to be on the property, not per the judge but per the asshole that lived in The House I Paid For.

August 14: I texted Glen to remind him the movers would be there the next day at noon.

Glen answered, *"August 15 is not an option for days to move. I sent you August 13 was the date"*

"This is the date and time you chose. They will be there at the appointed time tomorrow."

"I am taking vacation time away from my work. Have them bring me lunch. I & my employer do not like this time hostage on working with a short time frames to accommodate you"

August 15: Everyone arrived at the house at noon. Glen met them in the driveway and stated he had the stuff all set aside. He had a pile of crap, which did not include any of the things on the list, other than my father's large safe. So, I paid everyone to literally pick up garbage.

Glen told my representative that his lawyer told him he didn't have to turn over all that property because the divorce had been over since December.

To this point, this gaslighting event had been going on for eight months, but with only partial resolution, as I still hadn't received all my items.

Ultimately, I charged Glen with contempt of court because he was not following the court ruling. We went to court. The judge decided Glen was in the wrong and ordered that he pay for the movers and the items I had not received. Shockingly, he was not charged with contempt.

Additionally, in our divorce decree, there was a section stating that if someone didn't follow the stipulations, the guilty party had to pay the attorney fees for both parties. Not stated, but apparently implied, was that this did not apply to a strong, financially capable female. That person must pay her own attorney fees, even as the innocent victim. The unmitigated gall of all those involved in this blatant stealing from me!

Fairness is not to be assumed in court. As a result, my trust in the judicial system continued to dwindle.

❀

Now it was time for our first family function after the divorce. *Ughh!* I knew this was going to suck, and it did! It was Sawyer's high school graduation.

Sawyer and I decided that the church hall would be a good, neutral location for this event.

I reserved the hall, and we let Glen know the date and location. Three weeks before the party, Glen texted that he was taking the boys out of town on the weekend of the planned party.

I canceled the hall.

Glen unilaterally decided he was having the party at The House I Paid For and that he was having it on graduation weekend, which was during my parenting time.

Glen texted, *"Sawyer has told you that he will be with me for the graduation party all day. You have known about this for a long time now is not the time to have an argument about it the calendar will be changed."*

Poor Sawyer, he just could not figure out a way to make everyone happy. I took the high road and told him we would celebrate with my side of the family during our annual fishing trip. I watched the relief dissolve tension from his face and shoulders.

Graduation day came and I attended the ceremony, then went to my loft. I was so very sad to be missing a huge event in the life of my child. I got on my bike and took off down the bike path. My sister, Amelia, called me to see how I was doing, as she knew this event was happening. I stopped my bike to talk to her because I was crying so hard that I could hardly catch my breath. Amelia called Jenny who immediately called me and told me she was going to meet me at my apartment right away. Thank God for my family! Thank God for friends! They saved me on that day.

I will never, ever, forgive Glen for taking this day from me! Not ever!

❀

One Saturday, I was at the hospital on call. Molly was visiting me but needed to head back to her college town because she was leaving for a study abroad the following Monday.

She called me about midmorning to tell me that her car battery was dead.

She had already called Glen, and he was berating her and telling her this was somehow my fault. He would not come help her. Molly then called her uncle, Glen's brother, to see if he would come help. Her uncle called Glen and told him to go help his daughter.

Glen finally came to jump her car.

He told her in a text message, *"Your mom is responsible for all expenses relating to college until you kids are twenty-four. Since you need the car to get back to college, it is mom's responsibility to buy a new battery."*

Wow! Pretty convoluted rationale to avoid paying for his child's car battery. I had always told my kids that I would pay for their undergraduate degrees, which I did, but that did not mean I was responsible for everything during their college years, particularly to the random age of twenty-four.

❀

Glen refused to transfer Molly's vehicle title to her, which was a requirement per the divorce decree. He also refused to pay the registration fee, and since I was not on the title either, I was not able to pay it. After the plates expired, she could not legally drive her vehicle and that date was fast approaching.

Molly drove home to get the title, as Glen said he would give it to her personally rather than mailing it. She was used to this kind of manipulation and knew it was easier to agree and come get it rather than state the obvious easier path of using the mail.

Molly went to The House I Paid For and Glen was not there. She texted him and he stated that the title was taped to the mirror in her bedroom. It wasn't. She knew he would lie and say it was there, so she took a picture of the empty mirror and the surrounding area in her room.

He later texted her that he had gotten home and asked her why she didn't get the title.

Molly answered, *"It was not there."*

"yes it was on the mirror."

"It was not there" she texted and then attached the picture of the mirror.

"Send me a picture of your moms apartment. She is just trying to see what is in my house. She told you to take that picture"

Molly eventually got the title after yet another, exhausting gaslighting process.

❀

Glen refused to change Sawyer's vehicle title to his name, which was a court stipulation as well. This became tricky when Glen decided to drop Sawyer's vehicle from his insurance, as it is not possible to insure a vehicle when you are not on the title.

In his usual chaos, Glen texted me at 6 p.m. stating, *"Sawyer and I just realized his insurance for the automotive is over tonight at midnight please add them to your coverage"*

This meant I would need to drive them to and from school until I could get this added to my insurance. Since neither Sawyer nor I were not on the title, I had to go through the hassle of presenting the divorce decree at the state office.

He sent an additional text stating, *"I cannot add him to my insurance until you put Sawyer on the title. In the divorce you wanted the cars so now you have them and now you have the bills to go with them, I've always paid and take care of all the finances this is something you're going to have to learn to take care of I know it's new for you but you have to learn how to pay bills with everything that you've acquired during the divorce"*

Oh brother, so much wrong in just one text. I got one car. And the comment about him taking care of all the finances comes from the fact that he did physically write the checks, but with MY money. Oh, and I am so stupid that I can't possibly figure this all out.

I think the issues with the cars were based on his odd attachment to material things. He was unable to get rid of things. It was also part of his issue with control of all things involving me and the kids.

❦

Goldie, Hunter's dog, was stuck following the custody schedule with Hunter. Occasionally, Glen wanted Goldie when it was not his parenting time. Of course, I paid all the veterinary bills and bought all the dog food, but Glen felt he could take her at his whim. This was typically when he wanted her to retrieve birds during a pheasant hunt. No dog meant walking his lazy ass over to pick up the dead bird himself, God forbid!

Anyway, Glen showed up outside my house unannounced and texted Hunter to bring Goldie out to his car so he could take her hunting for the evening. I said no to that demand as Glen had always insisted that Goldie stay with Hunter wherever he was. He had started calling her a "companion dog."

Of course, he expected me to keep Goldie whenever he was going to be out of town during his parenting time, but I let that slide because I wanted Goldie with me all the time anyway.

Hunter went outside to talk to Glen and when he returned, he was very frustrated. This is when the harassment started, and my phone blew up with texts.

Glen texted, *"Hunter wants me to call the police because you will not let him out of the house. With Goldie is he in danger"*

I didn't take the bait and instead tried to ignore the commotion he was causing.

Glen's next text was, *"You are not letting Hunter talk to me on his phone or come outside and talk to me that is harmful to him"*

The gaslighting is apparent right away with this interaction as Hunter had been outside to talk to him and had also spoken with him several times on the phone.

He then texted, *"If he doesn't come outside in five minutes I'm going to dial 911 for a wellness check"*

Threatening to call the police was typical when he didn't get what he wanted.

Next, *"Why are you hurting Hunter's feelings"*

By this point, Hunter was getting more frustrated, and I didn't want him to be stuck in this interaction any longer.

I texted, *"Goldie is Hunter's companion dog per your words.*

She is staying here. Leave my house now."

His response, *"Hunter is upset how mean you are to him you're hurting his feelings you're not giving him the wishes that he wants you're a very mean and controlling person"*

Next, he texted, *"You should get the kids what they want in their going to end up hating you for ever. For what you did to our family and you're continuing to be controlling"*

He couldn't stop the vitriol, so it kept coming. His next comment is blatant narcissism as he texted, *"And this is things that need to be said so that you can grow and get better"*

I texted, *"Blah blah blah blah"*

"I feel sorry for you," he wrote.

"Blah blah blah"

By this point, I had a much clearer picture of narcissism and gaslighting. This interaction had started with a demand to take the dog and contorted into the implication that I was harming Hunter. A texting stream from him was never complete until he got his final licks in about my character and how I had ruined everyone's life by leaving him. It was also typical for him to end an interaction with some sage advice about how I could grow into a better person and "get better," because of course he always told me I was the crazy one.

Eventually, oh my God so much later than I should have, I blocked Glen's phone number. I didn't do this sooner because I rationalized that he might need to get a hold of me if there was an emergency with one of the kids. But, after repeatedly banging my head on the concrete wall with this texting abuse, I had an epiphany. I realized he would never let me know if there was an emergency with the kids. I actually had zero necessary attachments to this man.

And I finally, finally, ended the harassment by simply blocking him on my phone. This was immediately so very freeing that my shoulders physically felt a weight being lifted. I had carried that weight for too long. The marriage had ended long before this point, but this was the final disposal of the entire relationship. I obliterated his control over me.

Chapter 47

Do I Forgive Him?

I loved Glen, then I hated him, and eventually I "nothinged" him. I no longer reserve my heart and brain for him, and that has been very freeing. Other than the fact that he donated genetic material for the existence of our children, I have nothing at all to do with him. I am simply indifferent to him.

The question as to whether I can ever forgive him is a hard one for me.

I am aware that forgiveness does not mean what he did was not wrong, or even okay. It was very wrong!

I have forgiven myself for falling for his shenanigans. This was not that hard once I learned about NPD, as they are masters at manipulation. They understand the assignment!

I have forgiven myself for staying with him as long as I did, because I had no other choice. I could not leave my children alone with him when they were too young to defend themselves from his abuse or fend for themselves when he was not being attentive.

I have read that forgiving him may be better for me, but it appears the jury is still out on that. I personally can't understand how forgiving my abuser can help me. Is he sorry? Most definitely he is not! So, I don't understand how I can forgive him. I do know that I carry the burden of him within me and therefore remain victim to him, but is this because I have not forgiven him or because he abused me? He has no overt control over me since I divorced him and blocked him from my phone, but he still has subliminal control over a portion of my injured mind. My PTSD keeps him there. My newfound indifference to him helps me avoid reserving additional space for him in my mind, but he is still there.

I have forgiven myself, but that is all I can do for now. I simply can't forgive someone who took that much from me. If forgiveness is good for me, then maybe with continued therapy, I can give myself this gift one day. But today is not that day. Today I choose what I want and need as I continue my healing journey.

Chapter 48

I'm the Hero of My Story

My therapist often says, "You are the hero of your story."

At first, those words felt comforting—like a gentle encouragement I didn't know I needed.

But as she repeated them in later sessions, I began to sit with the meaning more deeply.

Her insights often come that way—seemingly casual remarks that carry profound truths, waiting for me to uncover them in my own time.

Several sessions later, after I shared the milestones I'd reached in reclaiming control of my life, I paused and asked, "Is this what you meant . . . about being the hero of my story?"

She didn't answer with words—just smiled with a quiet, knowing look that said, *Exactly.*

She brought me to the realization that I have courage, fortitude, and resilience, a few of the characteristics of a hero. When I look at my pattern, I do have courage during pain or adversity, and I do have the capacity to recover from difficulty. I don't think I would have described my younger self as a person with courage. I think that is because I didn't truly need to have courage until my Shon died. I felt protected prior to that time, by my parents and then Shon.

Shortly after Shon died, I remember a feeling of panic that I was on my own. Of course, I still had my parents and siblings, friends, and Shon's parents, but at the end of the day I was the one to sit with myself. I didn't think I could do it.

I was an unwilling hero of my story, as is often the case with people who are thrown into a situation that they feel they are not equipped to handle. A hero does handle it though. A hero rises up, in my case from the trauma of Shon's death and the trauma of marital abuse, to come out stronger and better on the other side. The other side, where I worked so hard to get and am so happy to be!

Part III

The Other Side

Chapter 49

Coincidence?

Almost seven years after the divorce was final, I took a two-week vacation to Siesta Key, Florida. I have never taken a vacation this long, and it was fabulous, except for one thing.

Glen!

Glen showed up not only in Florida, not only in Siesta Key, but on Siesta Key Beach! The beach right by my condominium.

Siesta Key is 1,678 miles from where we both live. There are three main beaches on this island, one of which is Siesta Key beach.

Coincidence? Of course not!

How did he even find me?

My children know to limit information about me when they are talking to their dad, but Glen had pieced together bits of information from each of them to figure out where I was going and when I would be there.

He allegedly had a work meeting in Orlando, Florida. I mean, who knows? He may have, I guess. Anyway, he rented a car and drove two-and-a-half hours from the Atlantic Ocean to the Gulf of Mexico, girlfriend in tow. There is nothing to do in Orlando or on the Atlantic side of Florida, right? Of course there are loads of fun things to do there, but I wasn't there to torment.

And seriously? With his girlfriend?

When Glen was on the island, it was during the part of my vacation that I was alone. Molly had been there for the first few days, and David, my then boyfriend and now husband, was there for the last few days.

So, I was alone on the island with my stalker.

While Molly was with me, Glen texted her repeatedly, asking her to share her location.

When I was driving her to the airport for her departure, her phone was going crazy with texts and she was obviously growing frustrated. I asked her what was going on and she said, "Dad is trying to find my location, so I denied it."

Unfortunately, despite her efforts to protect her privacy, and mine, she shared a picture on SnapChat, a social media app, and accidentally had her location tagged. That is how he knew I was at Siesta Key beach specifically.

Molly called me a few days after she returned home to tell me about her accidental slip with my location.

She said she figured it out when Glen called her after he returned home. He told her that he had made a great find: Siesta Key Beach!

He told her how he and his girlfriend walked up and down

the miles-long beach.

I don't know if he saw me on the beach. I didn't see him. Thank God!

However, on the day Glen was there, I stopped at a bar and grill to get takeout for supper. I was sitting at the bar waiting for my food and scrolling on my phone. I suddenly had the feeling someone was looking at me. I looked around for a couple seconds and then decided that it was unlikely as I didn't know anyone there.

Glen ate at that restaurant that night. He had told Molly that if she ever went back, she should go to that restaurant because it was so good.

I know this was my sixth sense. I felt the devil in my midst.

To be sure, he would not have searched this hard for me while we were married. Back in those days, he avoided everything about me but my paycheck.

Molly was horrified! It was very hard for her to come to the full realization of what her father was capable of.

Fortunately, when Molly called to tell me this had happened, David was on the island with me. As I became triggered, David stayed calm.

He said, "It is messed up that Glen came here, but you are fine. Moving forward, we will make sure the kids avoid giving him any information."

He validated my fear, reminded me that I was just fine, and voiced the plan. All incredibly calming and the perfect thing to say.

David is the turning point in my life story. Life was good when I met him, but this is when life started to be great again!

Chapter 50

Life Restarts

When I was growing up, I just assumed I would be married as an adult. I don't think I even put thought into this. It was a foregone conclusion, probably because marriage was the societal norm at that time.

When I was married to Shon, I loved it! I loved that someone felt unconditional love for me. I loved that I felt complete. I loved spending time with someone whom I thoroughly enjoyed. I loved feeling safe.

But during so much of my marriage to Glen, I fantasized about being single, because that seemed so much better than what I was experiencing. I did not feel unconditional love. I did not feel complete. I did not like spending time with him. And I did not feel safe.

But then, years after the divorce and with lots of therapy and self-reflection, I wanted to find love again. I realized I am inherently desirous of being with a person, my person. I wanted back what had been prematurely ripped from my grasp when Shon died.

In order to find my person, I had to be vulnerable: not my strong suit after protecting myself for so long. The potential benefit seemed worth the risk, but could I learn to trust again? And probably more importantly, could I trust myself to pick a man with the best characteristics for me?

I didn't know the answer to these questions, but there was only one way to find out. I mustered my courage and jumped back into the dating world. I had a few false starts with men who were nice but not exactly right for me, and then I met David. David, my second true love!

I met David the usual way for this era: through an online dating site.

David noticed my profile picture first, which showed me racing my Bianchi road bike. He is a cyclist as well, so this piqued his interest.

As an interesting side note, I had unsuccessfully tried to change that to a different picture the night before David saw it. I don't know what I was doing wrong, but I kept dragging the new picture to the spot and it wouldn't stay. I got frustrated and just left it. Coincidence . . . nope, just life playing out my destiny. A God wink for sure!

David messaged me through the app and said he was intrigued by what I had written in my profile. I checked his profile and there was no picture. Oh no! That was a problem for me!

It was hard to date online, and I had to have a sorting system. My technique was to avoid profiles without a picture, avoid profiles with a picture that included a dead animal, and to avoid men who couldn't spell. There was also the obvious avoidance of the seventy-year-old men with a cigarette hanging out of their mouths while taking a shirtless selfie in their dirty bathroom. Seriously?!

I told David my rule about the picture, and he answered, *"I don't have a picture online because of privacy concerns as I am a professional in this relatively small town."*

I responded, *"I get the privacy issue, but I need a picture."*

He directed me to his work website, where there was a professional headshot. I immediately looked and was impressed. He was very handsome and there was kindness in his eyes. I can't explain what physically made him appear kind, but that is what my brain registered with that one picture.

I laughed to myself as I was clearly showing my cards by messaging back after looking at his picture.

I texted, *"You obviously passed that part since I am back. LOL"*

We texted back and forth and decided to meet in person just a couple days later.

I suggested the wine bar in the lower level of his loft. This was a public place that gave us both the opportunity to flee if necessary. Again, you never know with online dating.

As I was opening the door to our appointed meeting place, I briefly panicked: *Oh no, what if I don't recognize him?*

I am an introvert, so walking into a room without knowing the person I am meeting is very unsettling. I slowed my breathing and decided that whoever greeted me when I walked in was likely him.

I entered and the owner, whom I had met a couple times previously, said, "Hi Carol!"

I confidently walked up to him, reached out to shake his hand and said, "You must be David."

"No. Are you looking for David?"

Oh God! Crap! Really? This whole dating thing is so unnatural at any age, but especially when you are well past your teens or twenties.

I sheepishly answered, "Yes, I am looking for David. Obviously, this is a blind date since I don't know what he looks like."

It probably wasn't technically a blind date, as I had a picture, but it is hard to identify someone when all you have is a grainy, two-dimensional photo.

The owner smirked and walked me to a table stating, "I will bring David to you."

"That seems like the best plan. Thank you!"

I nervously waited, while trying to look cool and calm. David was brought to my table, looking exactly like his photo, but less grainy and definitely three-dimensional.

I stood and gave him a hug. I am not sure why I hugged him, because I really was not a hugger at that point in my life. I was more of an awkward, stiff person when someone went in for a hug. Interestingly, and as a side note, I am now happy with life, and I am a hugger. A change in state of mind caused a change in my core habits.

David and I sat down and immediately settled into a comfortable, back-and-forth conversation.

He had a phone call scheduled with his boss that evening (and he still assures me this was the truth and not an exit plan) and we talked until the last minute. He then walked me across the street, in a raging blizzard, to my vehicle. We had already discussed that we were both driving to see our kids the next day, so he asked if he could call me during the drive. Of course, I said yes because I did not feel nearly finished with our conversation.

The next day, after work, I was grabbing a bag from my basement storage room to pack for the trip. I noticed water on my basement floor. I was relatively new to managing every single aspect of a house and my mind started reeling with the possible causes, all of which seemed insurmountable.

As I was trying to find the source of the water, David called me at our scheduled time. I told him I was not on the road yet as I had water in my basement.

His immediate response was, "I should have called and checked on you before I left."

This! This right here is what really drew me to him. He had a protective nature, and he wanted to protect me. Me! I was now someone who deserved protection.

At the three-week point of our dating, David dropped me off at the airport as I headed out to a medical conference. He got my bag out of the vehicle and leaned in for a hug. I hugged him, and with my mouth directly adjacent to his ear, I said, "Thanks for the ride. Love you."

Yes, that simply fell out of my mouth. It was so automatic, as if it was one of my kids dropping me off at the airport and I was telling them that I loved them. It was just a knee-jerk airport response.

I immediately realized what I said and pulled back from the hug, face to face with my now stunned boyfriend.

"Oh my gosh! That just came out!"

In a split millisecond, I had rapid-fire thoughts.

Should I tell him that I don't, in fact, love him? That seemed harsh, even though It was too early for me to know if I was even in love.

Would he flippantly say it back, just to decrease my embarrassment? I didn't want a fake I love you.

Would he just vomit and walk away?

Those words absolutely cannot be taken back. And they are so important, at the right time and not on the gum-filled sidewalk while harried travelers are rushing through the revolving door.

David did the best thing possible. He burst out laughing, all while maintaining eye contact as I stood there with a stunned expression on my face. I then started laughing too.

He got control after a few seconds and said, "Call me right after you get through security."

Ok, so he wants to talk again. That is a good sign.

I got through security and immediately saw that my flight was delayed for three hours.

I thought, *I can sit here for three long hours and incessantly perseverate that embarrassing scene in my head or I can dive into the deep end and see if I sink or swim.*

I called David and we both immediately started laughing before anything was said.

I then said, "Umm, my flight is delayed three hours. Can you come pick me up and we can get supper?"

He excitedly said, "I will be right there."

We were able to discuss what I said as a very natural airport good-bye.

In actuality, I think it was my subconscious (and then my

not so subconscious) mind telling me that David was special.

We continued to date and are now very happily married. Our relationship is very healthy and is mutually fulfilling. We make decisions calmly, after considering our individual needs and our needs as a couple. We grow with these decisions, which is in sharp contrast to my life with Glen where every decision was chaotic, emergent, and designed to meet his needs unilaterally.

David and I are a perfect match, just like the old match. com commercials. I didn't think this would be possible for me. I had already found one perfect love with Shon, so the odds were not in my favor. But this relationship has been easy.

With the first picture I saw of him, I recognized something in his eyes that portrayed kindness. And he is just that, incredibly kind. When he looks at me, I know he is hearing me and he is going to do everything in his power to make me feel happy, loved, and safe. I am safe and my limbic system is learning to adjust to that.

We love spending time together. We love talking, swimming, biking, and running together. We love spending the weekend running errands. We love to do lawn work and gardening together. We love cooking together. We love raising our nine children together. We are a fantastic team that is summarily better than the parts.

David is not intimidated by my first love; he embraces it. He knows and appreciates that Shon taught me how to love and be loved. Then I had searched out love again because I knew what I was missing. I wanted it back so badly. So badly that I fell for the wrong man in Glen. But I have found it again. I have found it with my eyes wide open from my prior experiences.

David and I bought a river birch tree for our front yard. David recommended we buy the tree with three branches at its base: one for me and my kids, one for David and his kids, and one for Shon. These three parts have been the basis for our life together, with firm roots that will continue to grow stronger. Since we believe in God, we are also aware of His part in our lives.

Chapter 51

The Cloud Dissipated

The cloud that was omnipresent in my life is now gone. I no longer have someone constantly dampening my spirit.

I am a good person. I have worked hard for everything I have accomplished.

When I graduated from medical school, my dad gave me a card, in which he wrote the following message:

> *Dear Carol,*
>
> *I want you to know how very proud I am to have you for my daughter. You have accomplished one of the biggest of academic challenges and you have done it under the most difficult of circumstances.*
>
> *Love, Dad*

As evidenced in this book, the death of my husband was not the end of my challenges. I know more challenges lie in wait for me, but I will attempt to handle them with grace. I have learned who I am now and that came with a new word. The word is "agency" and I have it now. I didn't have it before, but I have it now. Agency is the freedom to make your own choices to shape your future. I am no longer controlled by someone else. I hated not having agency. I didn't call it that, but it is a perfect word for what I lacked for all those years.

As I was living the part of my story that was filled with abuse, I was not heard. I was constantly interrupted. I adapted to using a maximum of five words to portray my thoughts, prove my argument, and relay my needs. I was trained, by the abuse, to be blunt in my responses. This has been one of the things I am trying to change. I have a lot to say, and it requires more than five words. I consciously decided not to be afraid of my voice, and I do not care if someone else is afraid of it anymore.

I recently received an anonymous gift of horseshoe earrings in the mail. No note accompanied this package, so I had no idea who they were from. I eventually learned they were from a new friend who felt moved by my story. It was a great feeling to run through my brain's rolodex in an attempt to unveil the identity of the gift giver. As I did this, I realized there were several options. We don't stop and evaluate who our friends are until we are in crisis, or we get an anonymous gift. I certainly took notice, and I appreciate every single friend. I couldn't have done it without them.

I have learned that my brain requires forty-eight hours to downgrade a major event into a passing thought. Fortunately,

I have siblings, friends, and a husband who will allow me the safe space to endlessly vent until this forty-eight-hour period has passed.

In the grand scheme of things, forty-eight hours is a short period of time, even though several of my issues have been massive in terms of hurt and intensity.

Chapter 52

Love Yourself

I wrote this book as a form of therapy for myself. I have always journaled in my attempt to get thoughts out of my head, where they perseverate endlessly. Journaling became a way to lend some organization to the chaos that was gaslighting. This helped me see that I was not, in fact, the crazy one. These very journals held my story. A story I wanted to own and control.

Glen had tried hard to control me, but real power belongs to those who claim their freedom. I don't feel my marriage to my abuser was without purpose, because I gained the very reason for my existence, my children. I also gained my power and strength of will.

I think of Newton's third law of motion that states: For every action there is an equal and opposite reaction. I know this is referring to opposing physical forces, but I can also apply this to the opposing forces of abuse and love. Does his equal things out enough for me? Maybe.

With Glen, my life was overshadowed by black clouds that stole my sunshine. Detangling from my abuser was an intense thunderstorm. I had to hold steady and weather that storm. But it was worth it as the rain refreshed my life and my soul. I now live in a calm, refreshed world that is bursting with renewed energy. I am growing in the sunshine. My personal cloud has dissipated.

My story that was once sad and unfulfilling is now happy and fulfilling and adventurous and full of love. I evolved from victim to survivor to thriver. I have friends and family who love me, but more importantly I have owned my story, learned from my story, and learned to love myself.

So there!!!

About the Author

Carol Nelson, MD, is a wife, mother of four children, and stepmother of five children. She is also a neurologist and has been practicing medicine for thirty years. She obtained her bachelor's degree in biology from the University of South Dakota followed by her medical degree from the University of South Dakota School of Medicine. She completed neurology residency at the University of Vermont.

Dr. Nelson is the owner of Nelson Neurology, PC, in Mitchell, South Dakota. She is board certified with the American Academy of Psychiatry and Neurology and is a member of the American Academy of Neurology. She is also affiliated with the South Dakota Medical Association and Physicians Protecting Patients.

References

These references were invaluable in my journey. I did not use direct quotes from any of the books noted below, but they served as my knowledge base as I wrote and healed. I owe so much to the authors who came before me. Thank you all for normalizing my experience.

American Psychiatric Association. *Diagnostic and Statistical Manual of Mental Disorders.* 5th ed. Arlington, VA: American Psychiatric Publishing, 2013.

Eddy, William, and Randi Kreger. *Splitting: Protecting Yourself While Divorcing Someone with Borderline or Narcissistic Personality Disorder.* Oakland: New Harbinger Publications, 2011.

Kübler-Ross, Elisabeth. *On Death and Dying.* New York: Macmillan, 1969.

Behary, Wendy T. *Disarming the Narcissist: Surviving and Thriving with the Self-Absorbed.* 2nd ed. Oakland: New Harbinger Publications, 2013.

Brown, Brené. *Rising Strong: How the Ability to Reset Transforms the Way We Live, Love, Parent, and Lead.* New York: Random House Trade Paperbacks, 2017.

Kozlowski, Lauren. *Trauma Bonding: Understanding and Overcoming the Trauma Bond in a Narcissistic Relationship.* 2020.

Fjelstad, Margalis. *Stop Caretaking the Borderline or Narcissist: How to End the Drama and Get on with Life.* Lanham: Rowman & Littlefield Publishing Group, 2013.

Kaur, Rupi. 2015. Milk and Honey. Kansas City, Missouri: Andrews McMeel Publishing.

Carpenter, Malcolm B. *Core Text of Neuroanatomy.* 4th ed. Baltimore: Williams and Wilkins, 1991.

van der Kolk, Bessel A. *The Body Keeps the Score: Brain, Mind, and Body in the Healing of Trauma.* New York: Penguin Random House, 2014.

King, Carole. "Life Without Love." *One to One.* Screen Gems-Columbia Music. 45 RPM single, 1982.

Gaslight. 1944. Directed by George Cukor. Written by John Van Druten, Walter Reisch, and John L. Balderston. Los Angeles: Metro-Goldwyn-Mayer.

Endnotes

[1] American Psychiatric Association. Diagnostic and Statistical Manual of Mental Disorders. 5th ed., text rev. (DSM-5-TR). Washington, DC: American Psychiatric Association, 2022.

[2] Centers for Disease Control and Prevention, "About Rabies," last modified June 24, 2025, accessed [today's date], https://www.cdc.gov/rabies/about/index.html

www.ingramcontent.com/pod-product-compliance
Lightning Source LLC
Chambersburg PA
CBHW030908120626
46554CB00001B/61